The Capacity to Sin

Volume II

Rayford Jones Elliott

This is a work of non-fiction. All scriptures were taken from the King James Version of the Holy Bible, except where otherwise noted.

CLF Publishing, LLC
www.clfpublishing.org
(909) 315-3161

ISBN# 978-0-9899408-6-3

Cover design by Rayford J. Elliott.

Printed in the United States of America.

Dedication

This book is dedicated to you, simply because you have picked it up and it is in your hands. From my experience with *Capacity to Sin Volume I*, I found many people refused to touch the book simply because the word 'sin' tended to frighten them away. Sin is a big part of many people's lives, and they have become complacent with their lifestyle of sin. Therefore, because this book is in your hands, I take that to mean you have an interest in learning more about sin and perhaps you may even want to find ways to rid it from your life. You may have undesirable habits, things of a sinful nature, that are holding you back or perhaps you want to break away from some small habits in your life or you want to know more about how you can help someone else who you know is bound with sin.

Again, to YOU I dedicate this book. I pray that you will find it to be very beneficial in your walk in life.

Preface

There are many obstacles in life that can keep the full benefits of God from us. This book has been written to address the biggest obstacle in our life that can impede us from receiving the blessings of God: sin.

This book is divided into twenty chapters that address sin. You will find that there are many repeats of certain kinds of sin throughout this book. This is because there are so many of the same sins repeated throughout the Bible.

This book is not designed to be read as just a story where it is important to start from the beginning. You can start in any chapter, and you will yet get the essence of the book's purpose. Moreover, this book fits in the category of a reference that addresses sin.

This is the second of three volumes; the third is yet to be published. The first and second volumes address sin that was committed in the Old Testament Age and how to deal with each form of sin. The third volume will address sins committed in the New Testament Age.

Table of Contents

Introduction

When man was created, sin did not exist yet in the earth realm. Man was made perfect in the image of God. But after the first man, Adam, and his wife, Eve, disobeyed God and ate from the forbidden tree of knowledge, sin came into existence for man. Man's first act of sin created the atmosphere: the capacity to sin by man. This capacity then trickled down to all subsequent generations of mankind.

Sin is the act that is used to destroy man's character, keeping him from his rightful place here on earth and from getting into heaven. Sin is any deed, action or words that go against God's instruction as inscribed in the Holy Bible. This act places man into a position to be condemned by God. It can destroy the very purpose for man's existence. Sin chokes and keeps out the spirit of God, which is the source of life and the force that drives man to eternity in heaven.

There are literally hundreds of ways to sin, but they all yield the same result – a ticket to Satan's kingdom. To truly understand sin, it is important that one understands its characteristics, its roots, its sources, its causes and effects as well as affects. Yes, sin has a character, which is reflected from its source: Satan.

Sin is predicated upon disobedience to God's Word. Many times, sin and disobedience are considered as separate acts or entities. However, one cannot exist without the other. If you disobey God's Word, you sin; if you sin, you are disobedient to His word.

As you study the Bible, you will realize what sin is all about. It is a direct attack on the spirit of God within you. When a man does not know God, he is automatically participating in sin. Sin can also be a part of Christians' lives who are weak in their walk with God.

In warfare, you can strategically fight your battles by knowing your enemy and his dwelling place. The Bible tells us that Satan resides in the air (Ephesians 2:2). Therefore, as air is all around you, Satan is in your presence at all times. This fact helps you to prepare for his attacks.

Satan's attacks have three objectives. One is temptation. Temptation is a tool Satan uses to get your attention. There are many tricks he uses to get you to yield to what he wants you to do; he uses deception, such as the lust of the flesh, lust of the eye, and the pride of life to lure you into his dominion.

To avoid these attacks, you should be made aware that God provides a way to avoid Satan's tactics and keep you from being consumed. He provides ways for you to remove yourself from divers temptations (Satan's attacks). One way God teaches us to fend off Satan's attack is stated in James 4:7: *"Submit yourselves therefore to God. Resist the devil, and he will flee from you."*

In this book, you will find Bible stories about how Satan used temptation to try and get people to submit to him. Some saints fell into his trap, while others did not. These stories will be addressed, and it will be explained how today you can apply God's strategy to resisting the devil in your life. After all, Satan is nothing but a paper tiger; you can easily defeat him with the Word of God.

The second objective of Satan's attack is actually falling into the act, thus committing sin. Satan rejoices at this point because he feels victorious. He may have won a battle at this point but not the war. This is why God sent our Lord and Savior Jesus Christ to redeem us from our sins. When you sin, it does not automatically put your name in the "book of hell's registration." Sin can be forgiven. You merely have to ask God for forgiveness. Thus, forgiveness can be seen as a tool that God has provided to directly defeat Satan's objectives.

The third objective is damnation in hell. At this stage, all three of Satan's objectives have been accomplished. Two opportunities in the first two objectives were missed: the opportunity to ward off temptation and to seek forgiveness for sin.

Hell is the final resting place for Satan's demons and their recruits. These are the ones who fell short of the glory of God. There will be no turning back. Thus, one will be condemned to hell and eternally burn in "fire and brimstone."

Because God allowed His son to come into this world, it is possible for you to be redeemed. His redemptive power allows you to be saved from the hand that is trying to snatch you away from eternal life in heaven and instead throw you into Satan's everlasting home.

If sin happens to come into your life, the scripture makes it clear that if you confess and repent, God will forgive your sins. Forgiveness is unconditional; there are no strings attached.

In the Bible, "sin" is mentioned 389 times. When it is mentioned, most of the time, there is a story involved. This book will share some of the biblical accounts of sinful acts. Although there are literally hundreds of different types of sin, this book will cover a portion of these sins and their effects. However, you will find a list of over four hundred types and causes of sin in the back of the book.

I pray that the reading of this book will be a blessing and spiritually uplifting for you. God bless!

Chapter 1

Purging Sin

The nation of Israel perpetually committed all manner of sin. They took their blessings for granted and used them selfishly. They forgot blessings are gifts from God and are to be used to glorify Him. Instead of serving the Lord, they began to serve themselves, which led to a corrupt nation.

The sinning that was going on in the Israelite nation brought on the wrath of God. God was so fed up with His people's actions that He deemed it necessary to bring punishment to them. He did not want total destruction but a punishment hoping they would come to a realization of the cost of their sins. His plan for their punishment was to allow their enemy (the Assyrians) to invade and capture them. However, because God is a merciful God, He wanted to give them an opportunity to redeem themselves. Thus, God needed a messenger. The messenger He would choose would carry the warning to the people; however, if they did not adhere to the warning, they would be required to deal with the consequences of their sin. God had already made up His mind that the prophet

Isaiah was the prime candidate to carry His message to the Israelites.

Isaiah lived in Judah, the southern kingdom of the divided nation of Israel. He had been a prophet under four kings and was a good servant of the Lord. He preached repentance and salvation.

Isaiah was informed, through a vision, about being chosen to carry this particular message to the Israelites. This was a profound vision because he had an encounter with angels (seraphim). After the vision, Isaiah realized he was being called by God to be His messenger to the Israelites concerning their sins. But he knew when God calls upon you to do His will, you must be clean (free from sin). You must be pure in heart in order to be successful in accomplishing God's work.

As Isaiah was a man of integrity, he did not want to take the role of a hypocrite. As a result, he admitted he had sinned. The specific problem he had with sinning was with his mouth. This sin was apparently a perpetual problem. Isaiah's confession is provided in Isaiah 6:5: *"Woe is me! For I am undone: because I am a man of unclean lips, and I dwell in the midst of a people of unclean lips: for my eyes have seen the King, the Lord of hosts."* He knew, to truly do God's work, he could not have the baggage of sin hanging over him. Therefore, he asked to be purged from all his sins. He wanted his sin purged from his life. He wanted to be successful in delivering the messages God assigned to him.

By making his request to be cleaned from his sin, it was done. The Word says it was done by one of the angels. The angel touched a piece of coal to Isaiah's lips. Immediately, the sin was purged. After the sin was taken away, Isaiah said in Isaiah 6:7, *"And he laid it upon my mouth, and said, lo, this hath touched thy lips; and thine iniquity is taken away, and thy sin purged."*

You should examine yourself to see if there is any sin in your life. If so, then you should have it purged from you as Isaiah did. Psalm 79:8 says, *"Help us, O God of our salvation, for the glory of thy name: and deliver us, and purge away our sins, for thy name's sake."* Call upon God to help you. Ask God for forgiveness of any sin you have. He is faithful and wants you to live a clean, righteous life in Jesus' name.

In order to do the work of God, it is important to know how you stand with Him. Of course, we all want to find favor with Him. Isaiah knew what his situation was. He knew he had sin in his life. He, therefore, knew he had to be cleaned before he acted upon what God wanted him to do. If he had acted upon what God called him to do without a clean heart, he would have been walking in hypocrisy; hypocrisy is professing one thing and doing another. God requires righteousness.

Like Isaiah was chosen and called, you have been called. Peter describes the chosen one in 1 Peter 2:9-11: *"But ye are a chosen generation, a royal priesthood, an holy nation, a peculiar people; that ye should shew forth the praises of him who hath called you out of darkness into his marvelous light: which in time past were not a people, but are now the people of God: which had not obtained mercy, but now have obtained mercy. Dearly beloved, I beseech you as strangers and pilgrims, abstain from fleshly lusts, which war against the soul."* Thus, you can see what God has done (called you out); it is imperative for you to operate according to God's values and principles. Purging sin from your life is the first thing a chosen person must do.

You cannot be effective in doing His work if your life is not up to God's standard. You are special in God's eyes. As a matter of fact, you are part of God's chosen people like Isaiah was. Today, purging sin from your life involves two actions that are necessary to meet God's standard. Unlike Isaiah, who had the angel involved in purging his sin, you have direct access to God via our Lord and Savior Jesus Christ. The first thing you must do if you have sin in your life is seek forgiveness. All have sinned, and God is merciful and graceful. He allows all the opportunity to seek forgiveness for committed sins. 1 John 1:9 explains, *"If we confess our sins, he is faithful and just to forgive us our sins, and to cleanse us from all unrighteousness."*

Following seeking forgiveness, you must repent. Repentance means to stop and turn away from a particular action. Repentance is your proclamation to God that the sinful action will not be indulged in again. Acts 3:19 (NIV) explains the effect of repentance: *"Repent, then, and turn to God, so that your sins may be wiped out, that times of refreshing may come from the Lord."* This refreshing that comes from the Lord means you are no longer entertaining the same old sin of which you were once guilty. Isaiah was purged, and now you can be purged from your sin, so you can do the Lord's will effectively and live a righteousness life.

Chapter 2

Adding Sin to Sin

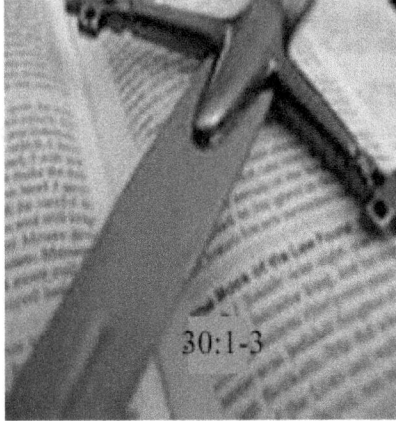

When Judah was threatened by its enemy Assyria, it recognized that it did not have the military power or discipline to go against its powerful enemy. They needed help. They had broken away from relying upon God for guidance and strength. The whole nation had become engulfed in sin.

The people were like a drunken man trying to read a sealed book. They did not know which way to turn. There was no spiritual understanding, and they did not worship God anymore. They had become completely reliant upon themselves; God had become void in their lives. When God is absent in your life, it becomes a life full of sin and lacks spiritual edification because you are no longer serving God. Instead, your life is lived in sin.

Because the people no longer served God, lived in sin, and relied on themselves, by default, they yielded to man for help when needed. In Matthew 15:8-9, Jesus uses Isaiah's description of the Israelite's rebellious attitude to describe the Scribes and Pharisees: *"This people draweth nigh unto me with their mouth, and honoureth me with their lips; but their heart is far from me. But in vain they do worship me, teaching for doctrines the commandments of men."* This is Jesus' quote of Isaiah's prophecy describing the hypocrites.

For assistance in facing the Assyrians, the nation decided to go to Egypt. However, Egypt itself was a corrupt nation and full of sin. They did not recognize God for who He is nor did they worship Him. They had their own pagan gods to worship.

Since Egypt was engulfed in sin, and the people of Judah were also corrupt, when Judah sought Egypt to help fight the Assyrians, Judah "added sin to sin." As Isaiah 30:1 put it, *"Woe to the rebellious children, saith the Lord, that take counsel, but not of me; and that cover with a covering, but not of my spirit, that they may add sin to sin."* Why would a man ask another man just as weak, or perhaps weaker than he, to help him fight his battle?

The scripture describes the affect and effect of the people of Israel and the Egyptians whom they sought help from when they failed to seek the Lord for their deliverance. Isaiah 31:1-3 says,

> *Woe to those who go down to Egypt for help, who rely on horses and trust in chariots because they are many and in horsemen because they are very strong, but they look not to the Holy One of Israel, nor seek and consult the Lord! And yet He is wise and brings calamity and does not retract His words; He will arise against the house (the whole race) of evildoers and against the helpers of those who work iniquity. Now the Egyptians are men and not God, and their horses are flesh and not spirit; and when the Lord stretches out His hand, both [Egypt] who helps will stumble, and [Judah] who is helped will fall, and they will all perish and be consumed together.* (Amplified Bible)

God expressed grief, regret and distress from the decision they made in their pursuit of Egypt's help. God grieved because He loved His people so much but found they had turned their backs on Him and let their faith in Him trickle down to a state of no trust in Him. God had time and time again expressed and made known that

He is the great "I AM," in whom all things are possible, and there is nothing too hard for Him. He would and could supply all of their needs.

Egypt had fallen down and had no strength. Why would the Israelites seek man's help when God was right there waiting for them to seek Him? The Israelites were no longer depending on God. But, with God's help, their victory would have been at hand.

Why put all your trust in man when he cannot help you? There will always be times when you need help fighting your battles against your enemies because your tools and weapons are just not sufficient to earn the victory. There are times you may feel equipped with the knowledge and skills you have accumulated. Sometimes, you may feel equipped with experiences in life. Sometimes, you may feel equipped because of your position in life. These things you may have, but there is no guaranteed victory with these tools. However, with God, victory is at hand.

There may be times when you will realize the need to seek help from others in your battles. It is okay to seek help from others, but not before you seek guidance from God first. *"But seek ye first the kingdom of God, and his righteousness; and all these things shall be added unto you"* (Matthew 6:33).

There is nothing wrong with seeking help from others, but if you do, use your God-given gift of wisdom to select a person or people who are strong in the Word of God and is/are living a righteousness life to help you to victory. This will fortify your chances of victory.

Do not make the mistake the people of Judah did: They lived a sinful life and sought help from their corrupt counterpart, Egypt. That is what a life of sin will do to you. Sin will cause you to look in the wrong direction and follow the wrong leaders to advance where you want to go in life.

The more one sins, the more one is inclined to reach out to others who sin. Thus, one is only adding sin to sin, which will make it harder to get back on the right track, the track of being led by the Word of God. Instead of taking guidance from those who would lead you astray, take counsel with God and watch Him work.

Chapter 3

An Offering for Sin

Isaiah 53:10 says, *"Yet it pleased the LORD to bruise him; he hath put him to grief: when thou shalt make his soul an offering for sin, he shall see his seed, he shall prolong his days, and the pleasure of the LORD shall prosper in his hand."*

The greatest act that happened to man was when God's son, our Lord and Savior Jesus Christ, came and gave a sin offering with His life. The prophecy that was made by Isaiah had then come to pass.

The prophet Isaiah described the coming of Jesus more explicitly than anyone else. His prophecy started in the last few verses in Isaiah 52 and continued into Isaiah 53. When man's nature had become a sinful nature and he continued to sin, God's abundant love for His children led Him to have mercy on them. His mercy was manifested when He sent His only begotten son to suffer, bleed and die for His children's sins. Through this, God made available for us direct access to Him via Jesus Christ to deal with any sin we may commit.

The prophet Isaiah prophesied Jesus' birth and death seven hundred years before Jesus' birth. In Isaiah 53:3-10, a portion of his prophecy described what would happen:

He is despised and rejected of men; a man of sorrows, and acquainted with grief: and we hid as it were our faces from him; he was despised, and we esteemed him not. Surely he hath borne our griefs, and carried our sorrows: yet we did esteem him stricken, smitten of God, and afflicted. But he was wounded for our transgressions, he was bruised for our iniquities: the chastisement of our peace was upon him; and with his stripes we are healed. All we like sheep have gone astray; we have turned everyone to his own way; and the Lord hath laid on him the iniquity of us all. He was oppressed, and he was afflicted, yet he opened not his mouth: he is brought as a lamb to the slaughter, and as a sheep before her shearers is dumb, so he openeth not his mouth. He was taken from prison and from judgment: and who shall declare his generation? for he was cut off out of the land of the living: for the transgression of my people was he stricken. And he made his grave with the wicked, and with the rich in his death; because he had done no violence, neither was any deceit in his mouth. Yet it pleased the Lord to bruise him; he hath put him to grief: when thou shalt make his soul an offering for sin, he shall see his seed, he shall prolong his days, and the pleasure of the Lord shall prosper in his hand.

So many today are wandering away from God's Word as sheep that stray. If you stray, you will no longer cling to what is taught by Jesus and the Holy Spirit. You will begin to indulge in fleshly things, which is not the way of God. There are many types of sins that are out there in this world that await you. But without dedication and obedience to God's will, like the lost sheep, you are liable to fall into the trap of Satan.

However, the offering for your sins has taken place. If you get trapped into Satan's web and cut off from righteousness, you know that our Lord and Savior *"was wounded for our transgressions, and He was bruised for our iniquities, and the chastisement of our peace was upon Him, and with His stripes, we are healed"* (Isaiah 53:5). What this means is Jesus has made available for you the opportunity to be forgiven for your transgressions and to have your iniquities blotted out. With forgiveness, you will be placed back into right standing with the Lord and again clothed in righteousness. What more can you ask for than Jesus coming and overcoming the world for you?

There are 107 references to "sin offering" in the Bible, and they are all located in the Old Testament. All reference an animal, such as a goat or ram. In the New Testament, there is only one sacrifice offered to deal with the sin of man. That sacrifice is Jesus Christ. His sacrifice was for then and forever.

His offering was a one-time act; that was all that was needed to make the way for man to enter into the kingdom of God via Jesus Christ. Of course, Jesus did say that no one can get to the Father unless they come through Him. John 14:6 says, *"Jesus saith unto him, I am the way, the truth, and the life: no man cometh unto the Father, but by me."*

Thus, Jesus made it possible for man to be born again via the blood He shed. No one can enter into the kingdom of God unless they go through Him. John 3:3 states, *"Jesus answered and said unto him, Verily, verily, I say unto thee, except a man be born again, he cannot see the kingdom of God."*

What God gave to us (salvation through Jesus Christ) is the greatest gift man has ever received. As God the Son, Jesus had power in His hand, but yet He opted not to save himself from His enemy, so we could all have the opportunity to be saved and cleansed from our sins.

The first man (Adam) was not created in sin, but today man is born into a sinful environment as a result of the sin committed by Adam. Jesus offers us, by God's designed plan, the opportunity to create in us a new nature through Him. This new nature is the indwelling of Christ in us. As Christ dwells in us, He begins to transform us into new creations. The Bible tells us to be not conformed to this world, but be ye transformed by the renewing of our minds (Romans 12:2).

Matthew Henry's Commentary explains what happens to all who receive and recognize what Jesus Christ did to open the door for all to be born again:

> Once one confesses with his mouth and believes with his/her heart that Jesus Christ died on the cross for us and was raised from the dead, he is born again by the spirit or has been saved.
>
> We must have a new nature, new principles, new affections, and new aims. By our first birth we were corrupt and shaped in sin; therefore, we must be made into new creatures. No stronger expression could have been chosen to signify a great and most remarkable change of state and character. We must be entirely different from what we were before, as that which begins to be at any time is not and cannot be the same with that which was before. This new birth is from heaven, and its tendencies are to heaven. There is a great change made in the heart of a sinner, by the power of the Holy Spirit.

Chapter 4

What is Our Sin?

There are times when we may not be aware that particular actions we perform are sinful. These sins could have either been committed by words or deeds. This might sound strange, but this does happen. For example, people engage in activities they are unaware are sinful. They are ignorant of the extent of their actions; thus, if they are approached about what they had done, they will claim what they did was not wrong.

In the case of the Israelites, they had been sinning for so long until it had become a way of life. They had sinned, and their fathers before them had sinned also. They, along with their fathers, were worshiping Pagan gods and did not truly recognize who God is and the power He has. They had done this for so long until they adapted to a sinful lifestyle. They literally did not recognize they were sinning. The priests and prophets amongst them would speak to them about their sinful ways, but the people's ears and hearts were closed to what the Word of God says.

Jeremiah, the prophet, was given the assignment to take a message to the Israelites about how their transgressions would be dealt with by God. As he was preparing to take the message to the people, God told Jeremiah what the people's response would be concerning their evil acts against Him. God's Words are recorded in Jeremiah 16:10: *"And it shall come to pass, when thou shalt shew this people all these words, and they shall say unto thee, Wherefore hath the Lord pronounced all this great evil against us? Or what is our iniquity? Or what is our sin that we have committed against the Lord our God?"*

The people asked Jeremiah after he had delivered God's message, "What is our sin that we have committed against God?" Their perpetual sins had tarnished the truth in their lives. They did not know the truth or maybe they pretended not to know what wrong they had done. They responded naïvely to Jeremiah about their sins. The Quest Study Bible (NIV) explains that the people were "influenced by false prophets over the course of time. The people had gradually become indifferent to their sins. Unaffected by the gravity of their sins, they could not see how their trouble had been caused by their own wickedness" (p. 1110). However, knowing or not, they were going to be held accountable for their sins. No sins can be hidden from God or shall be overlooked by Him. That is the way God works; He gives you the opportunity to live a just and righteous life. It is always up to you to live the way of life He has laid out in scriptures.

They were sinning, and God was watching every move they were making. Jeremiah 16:17 says, *"For mine eyes are upon all their ways; they are not hid from my face, neither is their iniquity concealed from mine eyes."* God is always watching what you do; if He were not, how could He know to make judgments upon your wrongdoings?

Judgment was to be brought upon the Israelites for their disobedience. God pointed out what should be done to them and why, in Jeremiah 16:18, which states, *"Before I bring them back to their land, I will doubly recompense and punish them for their iniquity and their sin, because they have polluted My land with the carcasses of their detestable idols and with the abominable things offered to false gods with which they have filled My inheritance"* (Amplified Bible).

They had forgotten who God is and His power. God wanted them to know Him and serve Him. (They were the chosen people.) Through their punishment, there was hope that they would again come to know Him. Jeremiah 16:21 says, *"Therefore, behold, I will this once cause them to know, I will cause them to know mine hand and my might; and they shall know that my name is The* LORD.*"*

Get to know Him, in the power of His resurrection and the fellowship of His love, and then you will not ask the question, "What is our sin?" Having a relationship with Him will keep you full of knowledge, fortify your understanding, and give you wisdom to help make the right choices in life according to His word. Once the spirit of God is in you, He will continue to reside in you as long as you continue the relationship based on His Word and not on a worldly disposition.

If one walks in the spirit then there will be no question such as, "What is my sin?" The spirit in you will fully guide you the right way and help you make the right choices in your life. Galatians 5:16 says, *"Walk in the Spirit, and ye shall not fulfill the lust of the flesh."* The spirit will help you keep away from fleshy things that have the sin signature on them. He will keep you from being ignorant of the sins you may potentially commit.

The people in Jeremiah's time were walking in the way of the world and not God's way. The spirit of the Lord was void inside them. They thus lived the way of the world. Ephesians 2:2 explains what lifestyle people will live if they are not adhering to the Word of God: *"Wherein in time past ye walked according to the course of this world, according to the prince of the power of the air."* The prince of the power of the air is Satan, who is the enemy of God. Anyone who lives according to the prince of the power of the air is a servant of Satan and not of God.

God made all of us, and He desires and expects us to serve Him and no other entity. His grace is rich in mercy, and He is more than willing to stretch His hand out to you and forgive you of your sinful ways if you seek His face. When He sees in your heart the sincerity of repenting from a sinful life and turning to a life that honors Him, serves Him, worships Him, praises Him and acts in obedience to His word, He is pleased. Psalm 119:11 states how you might come into the state of being the type of servant God wants you to be, so you will do all the things that are required: *"Thy word have I hid in mine heart, that I might not sin against thee."*

Chapter 5

The Sins of Judah

Burning the work of God

Judah committed sins that would make believers' hearts shiver, faces frown, and tears fall. Their sins were the atrocities of sin. However, the sins they committed were not new to them. They had been engaging and disengaging in sin for centuries. Their lives were like a circle – a point of location would reappear sooner or later when the circular motion continued.

There are varying degrees of the impact of sin on those who witnessed the sin being committed by the sinner. It is also true that different sins elicit different responses from God. However, remember sin will not go unaccounted. God responds to sin according to His will. There is punishment for sin if it is not dealt with properly by the sinner. Of course, the proper way to deal with it is to seek forgiveness from God as soon as possible and repent. He knows what you are doing.

The people of Judah provoked God to a point of anger. He said in Jeremiah 17:4, *"You have kindled a fire in My anger which shall burn forever."* These are the words God spoke about their lifestyles– Jeremiah 17:1: *"The sin of Judah is written with a pen of iron, and with the point of a diamond: it is graven upon the table of their heart, and upon the horns of your altars."* The sins they were committing provoked God to anger because of what they were doing. Their sins were so severe; God spoke the words of their sins that were being written into their hearts. This meant God and His righteousness were nowhere near their hearts, minds or lives. The people had no intent to turn from their sins. They had completely forgotten about God and who He is: the one and only great "I AM."

Their sins were so profound that God elected to punish them. They would not listen to His voice. They were too deep in their sins. Their sins were described in Jeremiah 2. They had committed two offensives against God. Jeremiah 2:13 states, *"For My people have committed two evils: they have forsaken Me, the Fountain of living waters, and they have hewn for themselves cisterns, broken cisterns which cannot hold water."* The people had forsaken God. They had completely turned away from Him and were living a life of idolatry, and they were indulging in many more variations of sin. They became a people of apostasy.

God was so angry with Judah that He pointed out explicitly in Jeremiah Chapter 17 what repercussions (punishments) would result for their actions. He explained what He would allow to happen to them. Jeremiah 17:2-6 (NIV) states,

> *My mountain in the land and your wealth and all your treasures I will give away as plunder, together with your high places, because of sin throughout your country. Through your own fault you will lose the inheritance I gave you. I will enslave you to your enemies in a land you do not know, for you have kindled my anger, and it will burn forever. This is what the LORD says: "Cursed is the one who trusts in man, who draws strength from mere flesh and whose heart turns away from the LORD. That person will be like a bush in the wastelands; they will not see prosperity*

when it comes. They will dwell in the parched places of the desert, in a salt land where no one lives.

Though the punishment and consequence for the people of Judah is explained in Jeremiah 17, their sins were written in their hearts. Today, if you do not trust the Lord or obey His will, you will surely have your sins written on your heart also. There will be neither security nor salvation unless you repent. Your name will not be written in heaven, instead it will be "Written in the earth" (Jeremiah 17:13).

Where are you written? Surely, you would like to be written in heaven. Luke 10:20 says, *"Notwithstanding in this rejoice not, that the spirits are subject unto you; but rather rejoice, because your names are written in heaven."* Or, you can be written in the Lamb's Book of Life as stated in Revelation 21:27, *"but they which are written in the Lamb's book of life."*

The people of Judah missed out on many blessings because of their sinning. This too can happen to Christians today if sin is a part of their lives. Verses 7-8 in Jeremiah 17 states,

> *Blessed is the man that trusteth in the Lord, and whose hope the Lord is. For he shall be as a tree planted by the waters, and that spreadeth out her roots by the river, and shall not see when heat cometh, but her leaf shall be green; and shall not be careful in the year of drought, neither shall cease from yielding fruit.*

By trusting in Him, believing in Him, honoring Him, worshiping Him and glorifying His name, the Lord will help keep you off the streets of sin. He will pave the path of righteousness for you to walk in His will. The blessings He has for you is without limitation. Live your life according to the Word of God. However, doing so may not be easy.

The apostle Paul gave a good example on how he struggled with sin in Romans 7. He pointed out the law showed what sin was and we are no longer under the law. Paul struggled with what he should do and what he should not do and with what he wanted to do and what he did not want to do. Paul was able to defeat the enticement of sinful things by coming to Jesus Christ and allowing Jesus to make a new creature (person) within him.

Everyone today is faced with making choices about whether to commit a sin or not. But one must get to know the Word of God in order to know what is right or wrong.

A most wonderful thing about God is there is very little He expects from you. Deuteronomy 10:12 states so eloquently what God expects from you: *"And now, Israel, what doth the Lord thy God require of thee, but to fear the Lord thy God, to walk in all his ways, and to love him, and to serve the Lord thy God with all thy heart and with all thy soul."*

Do not live the life the people of Judah lived at that time. Live your life with your heart full of the Word of God. Then, you can enjoy all the many blessings He has made available for you. Thus, your choices will make you a reflection of righteousness.

Chapter 6

Remember Your Sins No More

It is tragic when sin keeps you from being all God wants you to be for Him. God is love. He is your shepherd, no matter how far you may stray away. He is always willing to find you and bring you back through His grace. God wants to be your spiritual father if you accept Him unconditionally. When you sin against Him, it breaks His heart. However, that still does not damage the love He has for you.

God's love is like a marriage where a divorce is unacceptable. There may be a time in your life when discomfort, turmoil, or tragedy develops that will cause you to deter from what God is offering or has provided. But His unwavering, everlasting love will always be there for you. Of course, there could be a separation from Him, but He is always willing to receive you again, give you the comfort that He has for you, and bless you.

God is such a loving and merciful God. This can be seen in Jeremiah 31. In this chapter, God promises to restore His people to good standing with Him. The restoration that was to take place was not just for the northern kingdom (Israel) or the southern kingdom (Judah); it was for all of His people, whether scattered or not. The people had been in captivity by their enemy for many years, but God provided a road to freedom for them, so they could return and rebuild their nation as God had promised, to live the expected life God had set for them. This restoration came as a promise from God even though they were in the midst of their sinful ways. However, the people first had to ask for forgiveness and repent.

God's love is strong and mighty, but it should not be taken for granted. God explained what will take place in the restoration of His people in Jeremiah 31:3-6,

> *The Lord hath appeared of old unto me, he saying, Yea, I have loved thee with an everlasting love: therefore with loving kindness have I drawn thee.* Again *I will build thee, and thou shalt be built, O virgin of Israel: thou shalt again be adorned with thy tabrets, and shalt go forth in the dances of them that make merry. Thou shalt yet plant vines upon the mountains of Samaria: the planters shall plant, and shall eat them as common things. For there shall be a day, that the watchmen upon the mount Ephraim shall cry, Arise ye, and let us go up to Zion unto the Lord our God.*

A sound of joy is made when you know how great God's love is for you. What He did for His people then, He will do for you today. However, if you are living in sin, have committed sin in the past, or just thinking about indulging in a sinful act, remember God is always present (He is omnipresent). He is waiting for you to reach out to Him. His unchanging hand is always extended to you. Grab hold.

There is an important lesson we can learn from what God did for His people as He restored them. God took their forgiven sins and threw them into the "Sea of Forgetfulness" (Micah 7:19). He did not hold the sins against them. Jeremiah 31:34 makes it plain what God will do.

> *And they shall teach no more every man his neighbour, and every man his brother, saying, Know the Lord: for they shall all know me, from the least of them unto the greatest of them, saith the Lord: for I will forgive their iniquity, and I will remember their sin no more.*

Therefore, when you sin, God is available to forgive your iniquity and forget the sin you committed after He grants forgiveness.

Your first step is to seek forgiveness in order for this to happen. The disciple John explains the process. 1 John 1:9 states, *"If we confess our sins, he is faithful and just to forgive us our sins, and to cleanse us from all unrighteousness."*

Man, on the other hand, will forgive his brother but at the same time will not forget what he did. But when God says He remembers your sin no more, this is permanent. What you did in no way will interfere with what happen next in your relationship with Him. Romans 4:8 states, *"Blessed is the man to whom the Lord will not impute sin."* This means that forgiven sins will not be kept in a logbook or a database to refer to later. God keeps no record of your forgiven sins.

You can now see how God deals with sin. All believers should know what the Word of God says about how man should deal with his sins. It is great to know that once forgiven no remembrance of sin is kept by God. 2 Corinthians 5:19 states, *"That God was reconciling the world to himself in Christ, not counting people's sins against them. And he has committed to us the message of reconciliation."*

It is good to have a true relationship with God. Through this relationship, you will get to know Him more and more as you continue to grow spiritually. He said all will get to know Him from the least to the greatest: *"Know the Lord: for they shall all know me, from the least of them unto the greatest of them, saith the Lord"* (Jeremiah 31:34).

How well do you know Him? Are you seeking forgiveness? His desire for you is for you to love Him, honor Him, and worship Him in faith through a righteous life. With this type of life, God will allow you to receive all of the benefits He has for you. Psalm 68:19 speaks of the Lord's benefits: *"Blessed be the Lord, who daily loadeth us with benefits, even the God of our salvation."*

Psalm 103:2 also tells you that you should be encouraged and reminds you not to forget His benefits: *"Bless the Lord, O my soul, and forget not all his benefits."*

God forgives and remembers not your committed sins. Open up your heart and your mind to recognize the divine power of the Lord. Let Him forgive and cast away your sins into the "Sea of Forgetfulness."

Chapter 7

Stumbling Block Effect of Sin

You are taught throughout scripture that you are to live a righteous life, by living your life according to the Word of God by maintaining your obedience to Him. Righteousness according to His word is what leads you to eternity in His kingdom. This is your goal or rather should be your goal. You should resist the devil to achieve your goal because he (Satan) is the only obstacle that can keep you away from victory in life.

Righteousness is defined in Deuteronomy 6:25: *"And it shall be our righteousness, if we observe to do all these commandments before the Lord our God, as he hath commanded us."* Sin is what keeps you away from righteousness. Sin is like a "pop-up" on a computer; it displays its ugly head at its own opportune time to try to deceive you about making godly choices versus ungodly ones.

Once you come into the knowledge of the truth (Jesus Christ), you are to resist all temptations Satan parades in your face. Staying focused on God will assist in resisting the devil. In Ezekiel 3, God's people lost their focus on Him even though they knew the truth about God and the service to Him they were required to render as believers. Ezekiel took a warning to them from God concerning the punishment they would receive for turning away from Him. Ezekiel states in 3:20, *"Again, When a righteous man doth turn from his righteousness, and commit iniquity, and I lay a stumbling block before him, he shall die: because thou hast not given him warning, he shall die in his sin, and his righteousness which he hath done shall not be remembered; but his blood will I require at thine hand."*

A stumbling block is an obstacle that lies in the path causing a person to lose his balance or fall. In this case, it is an enticement to sin or to stray away from the way God wants you to live. When one encounters a stumbling block, it is also a test of one's commitment and the strength of his faith in God. With strong faith and solid commitment to the Word of God, you will not fall to divers temptations.

Everyone runs into a stumbling block at some point in his life. It is imperative for one to stay prayed up. So, when a person runs into a stumbling block, he is prepared to deal with it in a spiritual manner, rather than allow it to place him in a state of disobedience to God's Word.

When a man becomes unrighteous and commits iniquity, he has thrown a stumbling block into his own life. Sin could cause him to forfeit the blessings of God and hinder his ability to enter into God's kingdom. A stumbling block can cause him to miss the kingdom of heaven. God is basically saying a stumbling block may lead to one's death, which is a spiritual death - causing him to "die in his sin."

When a man has been living a righteous life and he turns away from it to live an unrighteousness life, all the good service he rendered to God will not be remembered or counted, unless he returns to God. This is because he has paved his way to Satan's kingdom. Actually, he is already living in Satan's kingdom because Satan's kingdom starts with sin.

Satan's kingdom perpetuates sin but can be overcome by reaching for the hand of God to pull you out. When evil prevails, you then live on the other side of the fence where Satan resides. Satan's kingdom is all about evil and unrighteousness. Ezekiel 18:24 puts it so clearly about what will happen when a man turns away from righteousness: *"But when the righteous turneth away from his righteousness, and committeth iniquity, and doeth according to all the abominations that the wicked man doeth, shall he live? All his righteousness that he hath done shall not be mentioned: in his trespass that he hath trespassed, and in his sin that he hath sinned, in them shall he die."*

The stumbling block of unrighteousness can be removed by repentance and forgiveness. This is what God has provided for you- His desire for you is righteous living by honoring and serving Him. God loves you so much and desires for you to live an upright and righteous life that He permitted His son Jesus Christ to be atonement for your sin. That - my friend - is love.

As you honor God and know how He feels about living a righteous life, encouragement will come to keep you on the right path where stumbling can be minimized or stopped altogether. Even though there may be times when you may be tempted to fall from your righteous living as though you have run into a stumbling block, you can respectfully say with the help of God, that you may trip, but He will not let you fall. This is because God is always there for you during the good and the bad situations.

Psalm 37:25 states, *"Yet have I not seen the righteous forsaken, nor his seed begging bread."* Psalm 9:10 states, *"For thou, Lord, hast not forsaken them that seek thee."* Psalm 34:19 states, *"Many are the afflictions of the righteous: but the Lord delivereth him out of them all."* The verses just mentioned should be enough to keep all believers walking straight in the eyes of the Lord. But if this is not enough, then let's see what Jesus did to help. 2 Corinthians 5:21 states, *"For he hath made him to be sin for us, who knew no sin; that we might be made the righteousness of God in him."*

There is always a capacity to sin, which means that all are born in sin or moreover, all are born in a sinful environment which was created by the sin of Adam. Although one is surrounded by a sinful environment, it does not necessarily mean that one has to participate or become a part of its characteristics. One merely has to hold onto God's unchanging hand, and He will keep him in a state of resistance from the enemy's temptation. My advice is to take the path to righteousness.

Chapter 8

Confessing Sin

Confession of sins is the pathway to righteousness. Once you have "become infected" or have committed a sin, the way to remedy this act is by confessing to our Lord and Savior. However, confession does not fix what was done, but by the grace of God, He takes your committed sin and erases it from your heavenly record as it is forgiven.

Sin is committed all the time, and it is always damaging to the soul. Sin destroys the soul and the very essence of why you are here on this earth. But, thank God for there is a way out of sin and its deadly poison. You live in sin, which means it is all around you, but scripture tells you that you do not have to yield to it.

Scripture also tells you in the New Testament that part of being saved is confessing your sins; the other part is to believe with your heart what Jesus did for you and come into repentance. Confessing sin is not a new concept with the advent of the New Testament, it was originally done in the times of the Old Testament. As a matter of fact, "confessing sin" is mentioned a few times in the Old Testament.

Examples are Leviticus 5:5 where sin should be confessed if any of the laws (laws given by God) were broken, such as touching unclean animals. Verse 5:4 states, *"If a soul swear, pronouncing with his lips to do evil, or to do good, whatsoever it be that a man shall pronounce with an oath, and it be hid from him; when he knoweth of it, then he shall be guilty in one of these."*

The laws were laid out for the people of Israel to abide by. In Numbers 5, God gave Moses commands for His people. They were in all ways to abide by these laws. If they violated these laws or sinned against the Lord, *"Then they shall confess their sin which they have done"* (Numbers 5:7). In 1 Kings 8:33, when the people of Israel were *"smitten down before the enemy"* and sinned against God, they realized there was security in turning back to God. However when they turned back, they were to "confess" their sins by His name, pray, and make supplication unto Him.

In Nehemiah 1, Nehemiah prayed for his people (the people of Israel) and himself for the sins they had committed against God. He "confessed their sins" for them. In Daniel, in the ninth chapter, Daniel confessed his sins. Like Nehemiah, he also addressed the sins of his people. Daniel sought forgiveness for them. Daniel 9:20 states, *"And whiles I was speaking, and praying, and confessing my sin and the sin of my people Israel, and presenting my supplication before the Lord my God for the holy mountain of my God."* Daniel knew the importance of confessing sin. Confessing is acknowledging, and it represents an admission of a misdeed or fault according to Merriam-Webster's dictionary.

Confessing sin is good for your soul. Without confession, as pointed out in the New Testament, one can lose his chances to eternal life. Jesus came into this world to remiss our sins through the shedding of His blood on the cross. He left the blueprint of how we are to live our lives here on earth. We are to follow His teaching and live a righteous life according to His guidelines (scriptures).

When the people, as explained in Mark 1, came from Judaea and Jerusalem to meet John the Baptist, John was baptizing them in the Jordan River and had them to confess their sins and repent. Mark 1:5 states, *"And there went out unto him all the land of Judaea, and they of Jerusalem, and were all baptized of him in the river of Jordan, confessing their sins."* They had realized confession was a way of cleansing themselves from a sinful life. But John took it to another level- not just confession and baptism, but repentance.

You are to thank God for His grace and mercy. It is by grace we are saved through our faith and not of ourselves (Ephesians 2:8). Thank Him for allowing us to confess our sins and for forgiving us. John 1:9 states, *"If we confess our sins, he is faithful and just to forgive us our sins, and to cleanse us from all unrighteousness."*

You will put a damper on your confession of sin if there is no repentance. God expects you to confess, but He also expects you to repent along with your confession. Repentance means you have turned away from your sinful ways: It should take you away from the circle principle – what goes around comes around. You will move in a linear line where you never cross the same point twice, and at the same time, you will move higher in your relationship with God.

Is part of God's goodness when you confess and turn around and commit the same evil act again? God is a merciful God, but if you continue to sin, you will sin your mercy away.

When you confess, forgiveness is given, and forgiveness brings on praise. Therefore, after you seek forgiveness through confessing your sin, you should praise God continually. As you praise Him, it will help fortify your faith. Thus, strong faith in Him will help you ward off the devil's tool of temptation, which he uses to try to get you to submit to him. You are only to submit to God.

Furthermore, if one confesses his sin and continues to sin, then his confession is nothing but an empty vase; it has form but there is nothing in it to show the beauty of confession. Thus, the confession did not come from the heart.

The Lord God is the God of truth, and there is no place for lies or deceit. Making a confession and turning around and indulging in the same sin you confessed is equivalent to lies and deceit.

Jesus explained the importance of repentance along with confession of sin. Jesus said in Luke 15:7 (NIV), *"I tell you that in the same way there will be more rejoicing in heaven over one sinner who repents than over ninety-nine righteous persons who do not need to repent."* 2 Chronicles 7:14 (NIV) sums it up by saying,

> *If my people, who are called by my name, will humble themselves and pray and seek my face and turn from their wicked ways, then will I hear from heaven and will forgive their sin and will heal their land, says the LORD.*

Chapter 9

Eat Up the Sin

Sin, the enemy of mankind, can be perpetrated by the least expected. Perhaps you all have known people who seem to have it all together in their economic, political, social, philosophic and spiritual life. All seems to be well for them. They are persons of status who have been successful in coming up in the ranks of life. However, this success they had is futile if God was not a part of it.

What is important in any success, victory or challenge is the role that you allow God to play in your struggle. All the successes and victories of the world are not as important compared to being obedient to the Word of God. The Word of God provides the spiritual support which is manifested in the natural man. What is important is the spiritual level of understanding and living according to the Word of God; that is what makes life worth living and knowing that God's grace is the greatest gift that a man can receive. Note- grace is not achieved but received.

Throughout Biblical history, you will find instances of great men of status who have been successful in things of this world and have recognized God as the great "I Am" but did abide by the principle of life God so prescribed - being obedient to His word and refraining from sinning.

A good example is in the book of Hosea. This prophet, like most of all prophets during the development of Israel, received a message from God to deliver to His people.

The Lord dealt with His people in this instance as a double-sided sword. He did not have to deal with only the people's unrighteousness, but He had to deal with the unrighteousness of the priests. The people were sinning every which way that existed. *"There is no faithfulness or love in the land, and the people do not acknowledge me as God. They make promises and break them; they lie, murder, steal, and commit adultery. Crimes increase, and there is one murder after another"* (Hosea 4:1-2, Good News Translation) – Just to mention a fraction of their sins committed.

There cannot be any excuse for sin when one knows the truth; sin must still be accounted for. However, a contributing factor to their (the Israelites) sin was due to lack of knowledge. Hosea 4:6 states, *"My people are destroyed from lack of knowledge: because thou hast rejected knowledge."* They rejected knowing who God is. The knowledge the scripture is speaking about here is spiritual knowledge, not from the lack of knowledge in general. The scripture says without knowledge, the people will die - that is a spiritual death, which means there is no access to eternity, God's kingdom.

The sad part about this particular situation is that the priests and prophets during Hosea's time were not providing the spiritual leadership the people needed. They were doing things that violated the instructions they were given to uphold and to carry out the Word of God. Most of all, the teaching of scripture and who God is was taught by the priests. That was their designated job. But they, the priests, became the other side of the two-sided sword. They were indulging in sin just as the people were. As a matter fact, Hosea 4:8 put it this way, *"They eat up the sin of my people, and they set their heart on their iniquity."*

'Eat up' the sin of the people means the priests were sinning like the people were sinning. They were not condoning the people's sin but were using the product of their sin to materially prosper from the sinful acts the people were committing. This is as true today as leaders in churches and in the world parade as representatives of the Word and use the Word of God to make a materialistic profit for themselves.

It is so tragic that the priests and prophets during Hosea's days became false in their representation of God's will. They catered to the people's idolatrous desires and wishes rather than adhering to God's wishes. They fed upon the sinful ways of the people instead of upon the Word of God and totally disregarded the expected way God desired for them to live. The more the people sinned, the fatter the priests would get in their indulging in sinful ways.

They became false priests and prophets. As they catered to the people's idolatrous desires and giving in to the people's wishes instead of adhering to and propagating God's wishes, they created an unworthy status to serve in such a capacity. They fed upon the ways of the people instead of feeding on God's Word.

Sin, as it applies to everyone, will not go on unpunished. The next two scriptures following the above one describe how they would be punished for their sin: Hosea 4:9-10 says,

> *And it shall be: like people, like priest. So I will punish them for their ways, and reward them for their deeds. For they shall eat, but not have enough; they shall commit harlotry, but not increase; because they have ceased obeying the LORD.* (NKJV)

Thus, you must always be sober and level minded about things happening around you, as 1 Peter 5:8 states, *"Be sober, be vigilant; because your adversary the devil, as a roaring lion, walketh about, seeking whom he may devour."* You must be level headed, be aware, be cautious, be observant, be diligent, be acute, and be serious about the things happening around you. Without knowing and abiding by the Word of God, destruction will come into your life.

It is imperative to understand the will of God. Whether as a leader or a follower, knowing God's will, gives you discernment for sinful acts, so you may avoid them. Allow God to lead in everything. The Word says in Psalm 32:8, *"I will instruct thee and teach thee in the way which thou shalt go: I will guide thee with mine eye."*

Chapter 10

Sin According to the Wicked

Wicked means "morally bad in principles or practice" (Dictionary.com) or having committed an unrighteous act. Wickedness is a sinful condition; it is extremely bad and unpleasant in degree and quality.

Wickedness did not appear in the Bible until its mention in Genesis 6. There had been sin prior to this occasion; however, the sin that was committed by the unsanctioned marriage between the "giant" and daughter of the world achieved wicked status as seen in God's eyes. This was the scene of unjust marriages that took place on earth after God created man.

Man at that time had begun to multiply on earth, and there were many daughters that were born unto them. At the same time, there were "giants" who began to marry the daughters when it was forbidden by God. When these unjust marriages took place, *"The Lord regretted that he had made human beings on the earth, and his heart was deeply troubled"* (Genesis 6:6 NIV). The wrath was brought upon man, and the Lord said, *"I will destroy man whom I have created from the face of the earth; both man, and beast, and the creeping thing, and the fowls of the air; for it repenteth me that I have made them destroy all of the creation."* The wickedness of man caused the destruction of the world via water (the flood).

Matthew Henry's Commentary describes the ways of the people during the time before the flood in Genesis 6.

> God sees all the wickedness that is among the children of men; it cannot be hid from him now; and if it be not repented of, it shall be made known by him shortly. The wickedness of a people is great indeed, when noted sinners are men renowned among them. Very much sin was committed in all places, by all sorts of people. Any one might see that the wickedness of man was great: but God saw that every imagination, or purpose, of the thoughts of man's heart, was only evil continually. This was the bitter root, the corrupt spring. The heart was deceitful and desperately wicked; the principles were corrupt; the habits and dispositions evil. Their designs and devices were wicked. They did evil deliberately, contriving how to do mischief. There was no good among them. God saw man's wickedness as one injured and wronged by it. He saw it as a tender father sees the folly and stubbornness of a rebellious and disobedient child, which grieves him, and makes him wish he had been childless.

But before this destruction took place, God's grace found its place upon Noah. Through God's grace, man was not destroyed completely because Noah was a man of God and was not considered to be a wicked man. As a matter of fact, scripture tells us in Genesis 6:9 that Noah was a *"righteous man, blameless among the people of his time, and he walked faithfully with God."* He loved and obeyed God. Thus, God assigned him to carry on and continue to repopulate the earth after the great flood.

Centuries later, after the flood, the wickedness of man's ways was again flourishing. This was specifically happening during the time of the prophet Ezekiel. The wickedness at that time was not unjust marriages, but it came in the form of sinners questioning God. The question was centered on whether God's justice is just amongst the righteous and unrighteous. Ezekiel 18:24 tells us, *"But when the righteous turneth away from his righteousness, and committeth iniquity, and doeth according to all the abominations that the wicked man doeth, shall he live? All his righteousness that he hath done shall not be mentioned: in his trespass that he hath trespassed, and in his sin that he hath sinned, in them shall he die."*

God is a god of love and of perfect justice, and His mercy endures forever. When a righteous man becomes wicked by turning away from righteousness to unrighteousness, he will die physically and spiritually. God does not wink an eye at those who willfully sin. As a matter of fact, willfully sinning is characteristic of a wicked person. God takes notes on what you do, how you do it, where you do it, and when you do it. Wickedness and sin cannot be hidden from God.

Ezekiel was a part of the exiled chosen people at this time under the captivity of the Babylonians. He took this message of righteousness vs. unrighteousness and just vs. unjust to show God's mercy. When a man turns from righteousness to wickedness, all of the good things he has done will not be mentioned, unless he returns to loving and serving God. Wickedness can overshadow righteousness, and the consequence is death. *"For the wages of sin is death; but the gift of God is eternal life through Jesus Christ our Lord"* (Romans 6:23).

A Prayer - The Whole Armor of God against our Sin

Because of what we are wrestling with in this world, we should put on the whole armor of God, which He has provided for us. Let us pray.

Heavenly Father, we are thankful for your mighty armor. We put on your full armor: We put on the Breastplate of Righteousness. You say in Isaiah 32:17, *"And the work of righteousness will be peace, and the effect of righteousness quietness and assurance forever."* We put on the Girdle of Truth; you say in John 8:32, *"And ye shall know the truth and the truth shall make you free."* We put on the Sandals of Peace; you say in Isaiah 26:3, *"Thou will keep him in perfect peace, whose mind is stayed on thee: because he trusteth in thee."* We put on the Shield of Faith, which protects us from all fiery darts of the enemy; you say in Romans 10:17, *"So then faith cometh by hearing, and hearing by the Word of God."* Thank you, oh God for your Word. We put on the Helmet of Salvation; we pick up the Sword of the Spirit. It is the Word of God that we choose to use against all forces of evil that are attacking our lives. We ask you according to John 14:13-14 to be our guard and shield about us. Take us underneath your mighty wings, according to Psalm 91:4. We put your armor on, live, and pray in complete dependence upon you. You are our fortress and our refuge. We pray in the spirit at all times, and on all occasions (Ephesians 6:10-19). Oh blessed Heavenly Father, to YOU be the glory. Amen!

Chapter 11

Find No Sin

The prophet Hosea was told by God to marry a woman who would be unfaithful to him and cause him many problems. After he married, his wife (Gomer) lost interest in him and looked toward other men. This story of Hosea exemplifies what happened to God's people. They lost their appreciation of God and all the things He had done for them. Their trust in and reliability on Him came to a stop. They began to trust in themselves and relied on man for their survival and guidance. They compromised their "Christian lifestyle" and became unfaithful.

God wanted His people in Israel (the Northern Kingdom) to turn away from their sins and begin to worship, honor, and praise and serve Him. But each time they turned away from Him, they became more persistent in their sinning. It thus became a hard road for them to turn back from because of their so-called pride and comfort that had developed within them. They became an oppressive people within themselves. The prophet Hosea received the message from God to admonish them of the necessity to turn back to God and to turn from their wicked ways.

In the example of what happened to Hosea and Gomer, Gomer left Hosea and ran after other men. Hosea, being the godly man he was, had a great love for his wife, so he went to find her to bring her back into his life. Because he was full of love for her and he was a faithful man of God, the wrong she had done was no problem for him to forgive and receive her back into his home.

That is the way God feels about His people: God is full of love and mercy and is always willing to forgive when one repents and comes to Him. Ezra 8:21 reads, *"The hand of our God is upon all them for good that seek Him; but His power and His wrath is against all them that forsake Him."*

During the time when the Israelites' heads were turned away from God, they became prosperous in their material possessions. However, their newly found prosperity was at the expense of their own people. They, like their enemies, began to exploit their own people for wealth. They had forgotten the most important possession they could have- spiritual prosperity – that is, riches in the Word of God.

Joshua 1:8 says, *"This book of the law shall not depart out of thy mouth; but thou shalt meditate therein day and night, that thou mayest observe to do according to all that is written therein: for then thou shalt make thy way prosperous, and then thou shalt have good success."* This good success is obtaining the spirit of God within you. 3 John 1:2 says, *"Beloved, I wish above all things that thou mayest prosper and be in health, even as thy soul prospereth."*

As the message was delivered to them concerning their turning back to God and repenting, they found no fault in what they were doing. Hosea 12:8 states, *"And Ephraim said, Yet I am become rich, I have found me out substance: in all my labours they shall find none iniquity in me that were sin."* (Note: Ephraim is another name for Israel. The Northern Kingdom was called Ephraim, which was the most powerful of the ten tribes in the north. In the same way, the southern kingdom was called Judah, after its most powerful tribe.)

The Israelites were saying what they had done to obtain their prosperity was not sinful; it was a result of their own work.

Exploiting others for personal gain is a sinful act. They had turned so far from God that they had forgotten the basic principle of distinguishing right from wrong. They could not find any sin in their actions; that is the lifestyle of a wicked man. A wicked man will find no fault or wrong in what he does because he is out of the domain of the kingdom of God.

They had no remorse for what they had done. Right or wrong was up for grabs for them. Whatever they did that benefited themselves, they did it regardless of how it affected their relationship with God. They were like the people in the book of Judges; they did whatever they felt like doing. Judges 21:25 says, *"Everyone did what was right in his own eyes."* Their lack of spiritual discernment was from their lack of prayer and adhering to the Word of God, which was available for all.

Discernment means to look beneath the surface to find the truth. Discernment comes from God. It is achieved through prayer and studying the Word of God daily.

It is common today for the rich to claim that all they have materially accomplished is due to their hard work, their commitment, their intelligence, and their initiative. Sure, these things are relevant in achieving success, but without God, there is a void, a missing link to the joy, peace, happiness and fulfillment of life that goes along with success or victory.

They did not feel the need for God in their lives. But with God, there is so much more to accomplish in life. Not just materialistically, but mentally, physically, physiologically, and above all spiritually. All earthly things are temporary. But a good relationship with God can carry you through this world successfully and beyond this world to eternity where all things last forever.

If you find yourself doing something that you are not sure whether is sinful or not, pray to God and ask for wisdom and a discerning spirit. Pray and be of service to God. Pray before you do anything in this world. But service and prayer are incomplete without the knowledge of God.

God will supply you the opportunities, resources, and abilities to be victorious in life without the expense of others in the form of exploitation. You must hold your abilities and gifts He gives you sacred. Before you profess there is no fault in what you are doing, pray and ask God for wisdom. He will give you the discernment to assess the situation. *"If any of you lack wisdom, let him ask of God, that giveth to all men liberally, and upbraideth not; and it shall be given him. But let him ask in faith, nothing wavering. For he that wavereth is like a wave of the sea driven with the wind and tossed"* (James 1:5-6).

God will supply all of your needs. Philippians 4:19 says, *"But my God shall supply all your need according to his riches in glory by Christ Jesus."*

Chapter 12

Sin More and More

Once a sin is committed and it is not dealt with properly according to the Word of God, the wrath of God or anger of God can come upon you. However, means have been provided by our Lord and Savior to deal with sin before the effect of His wrath comes upon you. If you neglect to deal with your sin in the realm of God's guidance, you will find yourselves in a perpetual sinful state; that is, you will begin to sin more and more. This is what happened to the people of Ephraim.

God had already provided for the people of Israel. He had saved them from Egypt and from being in the wilderness. He had also saved them from their enemy the Assyrians. But after all He had done, they still lost their trust and faith in Him. Their sins against God became ongoing.

They consequently began serving the pagan gods they had made out of silver and other precious metals. They again did what their forefathers had done on their way to the Promise Land.

Israel had gone through the fire many times, and they had become a great nation with the guidance and help of God. Like the Israelites, today some believers' faith and trust can be easily damaged because they are not rooted deep and strong enough in God's Word. This is what happened to the people of Israel; they let their riches become their means to disobedience. Therefore, they rebelled against God. This rebellion against God brought defeat into their lives. They lost their authority among many nations and damaged their spiritual relationship with God.

They built molten images and began to worship them. This was to no avail because idol gods, such as Baal and man-made images made of precious metal, had no power no matter how much one worshiped it; God has all power. God is sovereign and has all power in His hands, which can be used to take care of all areas of your life if you honor, serve and worship Him.

The Israelites continued to sin over and over again with no remorse. The scripture tells how their sin was manifested as they continued to disrespect God. Hosea 13: 2 says, *"And now they sin more and more, and have made them molten images of their silver, and idols according to their own understanding, all of it the work of the craftsmen: they say of them, Let the men that sacrifice kiss the calves."* Making their pagan images was not enough; they went on to "kiss the calves." Their commitment to God was lost, and they continued to sin "more and more." Sin without ceasing is in essence an abomination to God.

Their sins were manifested in several ways. First, they boasted about being rich. All of the boasting was just empty boasts, and they were just "blowing off wind." Their riches and the way they obtained it were just temporary because God was not a part of it - only the things of God are everlasting.

The second manifestation of their sin was ingratitude. They forgot where their source of survival comes from and that there is great glory in serving and maintaining a righteous relationship with God. They forgot God had chosen them. Deuteronomy 7:6 states,

"For thou art an holy people unto the LORD thy God: the LORD thy God hath chosen thee to be a special people unto himself, above all people that are upon the face of the earth." God delivered them from Egypt, fed them, sheltered them, taught them, and protected them, yet they showed no gratitude.

The third manifestation of their sin was a hardened heart. They followed their own plan and gave no thought to God's plan for them or His will. God had a tender heart for them. Nevertheless, everything they did was according to their ways and thoughts. But He knew all they were doing. God is omniscient. Jeremiah 1:5 says, *"Before I formed thee in the belly I knew thee; and before thou camest forth out of the womb I sanctified thee, and I ordained thee a prophet unto the nations."*

No matter how one gets caught up in sin, God is a merciful god. One may continue to sin, but God has made a way of reconciliation; that is through repentance. God is always available.

The people at this time had yielded unto divers temptations and allowed the enemy to overtake them in their lifestyle. All the time God was available to bring them out of their sinful state. Hosea 13:9 says, *"O Israel, thou hast destroyed thyself; but in me is thine help."*

One cannot continue to go on sinning without paying the price. The ultimate price for sin is the door of hell will open to receive you. Hell is the ultimate price for unrighteousness, but the ultimate price for righteousness is eternity with our Lord. Righteousness is what our Lord and Savior Jesus Christ brought to the table for us; you can take it or leave it. Sinning more and more or continuously can be cancelled out by righteous living according to God's Word.

God is a merciful God, and through Jesus, He has made it possible to overcome unrighteous living. God is merciful to forgive your sins. To continue in sin, sin will open up the doors for more sin. Sin is like a "little white lie." If you tell one, it will lead to many more lies. Stay in tune with the Word of God, so you can hear and act upon His word. If you have an ear, listen to what the spirit (Word) is saying (revelation), so you can get guidance in living the life God desires for you to live.

Chapter 13

Altars to Sin

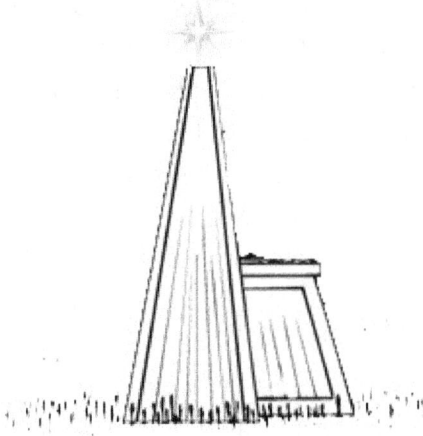

When man forgets about the creator and begins to worship created things, his life is destined for destruction. In the case of the Israelites, during the time of the prophet Hosea, this was their situation. They had taken their riches of silver and gold and made altars that did not represent the creator, God. They made these counterfeit altars and worshiped them, instead of God. In essence, they took away their focus on God via pagan altars. Thus, by not recognizing God for who He is, their life was destined to suffer disadvantageous consequences. Not worshiping God can cause a void in one's life and a lack of support through one's tribulation.

Hosea 8:11 explains, *"Because Ephraim hath made many altars to sin, altars shall be unto him to sin."* This act was contrary to what their forefathers always did. When their forefathers built an altar, they built it unto God; their altar was symbolic of worshiping God only.

For example, an altar was built by Abraham in Hebron, and it was built unto the Lord (Gen. 9:13-18). Moses built an altar and called it the Jehovah Nissi (Exodus 1:15). Aaron built an altar unto the Lord (Exodus 23:140). Joshua built an altar unto the Lord God of Israel in Mount Ebal (Joshua 22:10). Samuel and David built altars unto the Lord. Also noted in the Old Testament, there were many more altars that were built unto the Lord. These altars were built in remembrance of God and the things He had done for them – for they knew the pagan gods had nothing to offer.

The biggest mistake the people made during this period was to build altars not in the name of the Lord or to honor God, but to represent themselves. Through the glorified altars they made, they glorified man and neglected to see God as the only one whom believers should glorify, worship, praise and honor, because He is the creator and provider.

Warren Wiersby in *Bible Commentary* explains so elegantly that in Israel the 'trumpet' was blown by God to warn the people of their sinful ways. The warning was that the Assyrians were coming because of the Israelites continued indulgence in sin, and there would be no escape. Israel claimed to know God, but yet they continued to disobey Him and continue in Pagan worship.

"Israel had become like a piece of junk pottery on the trash heap. They trusted the Gentile nations to protect them and completely left God out of their plans. Israel multiplied altars, and Judah multiplied fortifications, but neither could deliver them from judgment. Israel would be taken by Assyria and Judah by Babylon, and God's judgment would fall on a sinful people" (Wiersby, 1991, p. 575).

All throughout history, as man indulged in apostasy (in and out of sinning), has always made some form of object to worship in reference to or to what he is indulging in. Sinners use idols and altars to customize their faith in the Lord, which is to no avail because only through genuine worship of the Lord there are blessings to receive and to open the door to God's kingdom.

Anytime the Word of God is counterfeited, such as building altars to one's self, a hypocritical act has been committed. There is no place in God's kingdom for this type of action. Altars can be made to satisfy one's own satisfaction but not God's. God expects all of His children to worship Him in the fashion He so designed, not by man's own creation. There is no reverence to God when this happens.

What all believers should do when they are in sin is to listen when God blows the "trumpet" and gives warning signs; there are always signs and wonders. Open your heart and listen to what His word is telling you.

Sin does not produce very good results. As a matter of fact, life is subject to destruction and sins provide a ticket earned to the gates of hell. Israel was placed in captivity by the Assyrians for their unfaithfulness and ungodly deeds through worshiping pagan altars that were constructed out of pride and blindness to the Word of God and not living the type of life He wanted them to live.

Altars were built in reference to worshiping God originally in the Old Testament. As a matter of fact, in Genesis 12:7, when God instructed Abraham to build an altar, this altar was to be built unto the Lord, and there Abraham would find His presence. There is no presence of God on counterfeit altars. His altar was used for praying and worshiping and remembering His promises. This was a way of symbolizing communion with God. Though many religions build altars for sacrifices, for God's people, the altar was built for worshiping and recognizing the presence of God.

In today's society, altars are not built in the sense that they were then; however, altars can be found in today's churches. An altar generally is located in front of the pulpit. This area is considered a sacred place in the church. This is a place where special communing with God takes place, in particular after the pastor does an "altar call," which leads people in accepting Jesus Christ as their Lord and Savior.

However, you do not need altars to worship God. You can worship God anywhere, at any time, or any place.

Jesus is an example of how God should be worshiped. Jesus found a quiet place and prayed. Christians too should find a quiet place, pray and worship Him. You can let your knees be an altar unto God. Bow to Him on your knees and lift up your hands and glorify Him. You can worship Him anywhere, anyplace and anytime the Spirit comes upon you. Amen.

Chapter 14

All Have Sinned

Nehemiah was a man of prayer and a strong believer. He believed in God, His promises, His forgiving of sin, and His great provisions. Like Ezra and Daniel, Nehemiah did not hesitate to ask God for forgiveness when he committed a sin.

These were great men of God who set an example for believers who get off track in some way and get locked into sinful living. Believers should understand and know from their hearts that God is the solution to sin. There is a way to atone for sin by asking and seeking forgiveness; the grace of God is always available to make this happen. However, in order for this to happen, one must acknowledge and confess his sins without hesitation.

That is what these three great men of God, Nehemiah, Ezra, and Daniel, did. They did this through their prayer. Nehemiah 1:6 says, *"Let thine ear now be attentive, and thine eyes open, that thou mayest hear the prayer of thy servant, which I pray before thee now, day and night, for the children of Israel thy servants, and confess the sins of the children of Israel, which we have sinned against thee: both I and my father's house have sinned."* Nehemiah interceded for the people of Israel, confessed the sins for the nation, and sought mercy for them through his prayer.

The notable part of his prayer was that he not only confessed his people's sins, but he also confessed his own sins; the depth of his prayer went even deeper because he prayed and confessed his father's sins. Nehemiah was a humble person. He could not just seek God's mercy for himself, but he also sought God's mercy for his people for the sins they had committed.

Confessing sin opens the door for forgiveness. All believers should be familiar with this path. It is available for all.

Hezekiah also made confessions of sin for his people after he became king. 2 Chronicles 26:6 says, *"For our fathers have trespassed, and done that which was evil in the eyes of the LORD our God, and have forsaken him, and have turned away their faces from the habitation of the LORD, and turned their backs."*

Ezra made a confession of sin in Ezra 10:1: *"Now when Ezra had prayed, and when he had confessed, weeping and casting himself down before the house of God, there assembled unto him out of Israel a very great congregation of men and women and children: for the people wept very sore."*

Daniel made a confession of sin in Daniel 9:20: *"And whiles I was speaking, and praying, and confessing my sin and the sin of my people Israel, and presenting my supplication before the LORD my God for the holy mountain of my God."* Daniel made confessions for himself and for his people.

These great believers, Nehemiah, Ezra, Daniel and Hezekiah, understood that dealing with sin is to acknowledge and confess thy sin. This is imperative because all have sinned. As stated in Roman 3:23, *"For all have sinned, and come short of the glory of God."* There is no exception among believers.

Once one has confessed and repented, it is important to know that the scriptures tell you that one does not have to fall back into a sinful lifestyle. It is a matter of making the right choices. 1

Corinthians 10:13 states, *"There hath no temptation taken you but such as is common to man: but God is faithful, who will not suffer you to be tempted above that ye are able; but will with the temptation also make a way to escape, that ye may be able to bear it."*

Confront Sin

Through the night, through the day,
The sin in my life oh Lord is for you to take.
As I walk through this life,
I am covered with your advice.
As I go with poise and the will to be strong,
I look forward to the day I will meet you home.
As I confront all of life's vices,
I have made my life a living sacrifice.
As I learn to do thy will,
I promise I will never be still.
As I become full of you,
There is no problem in knowing the right thing to do.
As time goes and I remain here,
I will go through life without any fear.
As the sins of life attempt to hit me hard,
I lift up my shield, the Word of God.
As I go into battle against all kinds of sin,
I am confident in you that I will win.
I see the goodness of you within.
I surely know I do not have to sin.
Though you make my sin as white as snow,
I strive in life to sin no more.

Chapter 15

Hiding Your Sin

Children's Bible Story Books. Lavistachurchofchrist.org

Your sin and iniquity cannot be hidden from God. Sin is recorded. One can go on sinning in his life thinking he can get away with it. But while it can be hidden from man, it cannot be hidden from God. All the unforgiven sins will be accounted for. God is omnipresent, and He knows everything that happens in your life.

Jonah is a good example of someone trying to hide his sin. Jonah was told by God to go to Nineveh and tell the people about their wickedness and the consequences if they did not repent from their sinful ways and live a godly life.

Jonah made judgments upon the Ninevite people and decided not to deliver the message God had given him. He disobeyed God and fled in a different direction. His disobedience led him to Tarshish and down to Joppa where he bought himself a ticket and boarded a ship to a different destination away from Nineveh.

After the ship had begun its sail to Tarshish, a tempestuous storm came. God sent out a great wind into the sea, and there was a great tempest, and the ship was destined to be broken up. The ship-mates became afraid because they had never experienced a storm like that one. The captain of the ship summoned everyone and wanted to know whose god was causing the great storm. They accused Jonah, as the one responsible for the storm.

Jonah was asleep in the bottom of the boat thinking he could hide and get away from God. God was and is in control of all the things that were/are happening; He had sent the wind, the waves and the rain. The captain was afraid and eager to know whose god was causing the great turbulence.

The captain found Jonah and asked him about his god; Jonah told the captain his god is the father of Abraham, Isaac and Jacob. He is the one who created man and the one whom all should obey. He knew trying to run away because of his prejudice toward the Ninevites would not stand. Because of his disobedience and trying to hide from God, God allowed the crew to toss Jonah overboard. As a result, he landed in the belly of a big fish and remained there for three days.

There is no hiding sin and iniquity because God knows everything we do. The people of Ephraim thought they were hiding their sin. Hosea 13:12 states, *"The iniquity of Ephraim is bound up; his sin is hid"* (American Standard Version). *"Ephraim's guilt has been collected, and his sin has been stored up for punishment"* (New Living Translation). But God knows when you sin and when you do right. If you do good, God knows, and if you do badly, God knows. There is no hiding place. You can keep silent about your sin or you can even forget about the sin you have done, but God knows.

Job addressed hiding sin, for he knew God was always watching. He states in Job 31:33, *"If I have concealed my sin as people do, by hiding my guilt in my heart."* Job was really speaking on hiding the sins he was accused of from families and friends because he felt he would be chastised by them. Because of the peculiar situation Job was in via God's involvement, he was blamed for his sin. However, he cleared himself in the following seven verses by confessing his sin to God:

Because I was afraid of all the people, and of families who hated me? Did I keep quiet and not go out of the door? If only I had one to hear me! See, here my name is written. Let the All-powerful answer me! May what is against me be written down! For sure I would carry it on my shoulder. I would tie it around my head like a crown. I would tell Him the number of my every step. I would come near Him like a prince. "If my land cries out against me and the ditches made by the plow cry together, if I have eaten its fruit without paying for it, and caused its owners to die, let thorns grow instead of grain. And let weeds with a bad smell grow instead of barley." (Job 34-40 New Life Version)

You cannot hide your sins from God.

Adam is another example of someone trying to hide his sin. After Adam sinned (the first sin of man) by eating the forbidden fruit from the tree of life, he tried to get away with it by hiding from God. Geneses 3:8-9 state, *"Then the man and his wife heard the sound of the LORD God as he was walking in the garden in the cool of the day, and they hid from the LORD God among the trees of the garden. But the LORD God called to the man."* Adam answered God while he was hiding and said in Genesis 3:10, *"I heard you in the garden, and I was afraid because I was naked; so I hid."* Note- his hiding was not only due to his nakedness. It could have also been due to his sin or disobedience to God being uncovered. You cannot hide from your sin!

The New Testament records Jesus meeting with His disciples at what is known as the last supper. He met with the disciples to give them a status report of what was going on at that time. Jesus pointed out to them He had been betrayed.

One of them who sat at the table had betrayed Him. He did not say who had betrayed him, but He wanted the culprit to know that He knew: What a great example of one of the characteristics of

God – He is omnipresent and omniscient, so He knows all things whether He is told by man or not.

Judas, the one who was the betrayer, was sitting at the table. One can image what Judas must have felt; there he was thinking his sin, which he had committed against Jesus, could be hidden. He was thinking he could walk away from their meeting free with no one knowing what he had done. There is no hiding sin from God!

The correct and the most holy thing you can do when you have sinned is to face God and confess to Him. 1 John 1:9 makes it clear and simple what you should do. This verse says, *"If we confess our sins, he is faithful and just to forgive us our sins, and to cleanse us from all unrighteousness."*

Confess your sin to God. He is the only one who can forgive you for your sin, not man, not family, not friends, not parents, only God. He is the one who has the power of forgiveness.

You can always open your ears and hear God's loving call to repentance. Once you return to Him, His arms are open to receive you back into His loving kingdom. Because His mercy is full of love for you no matter what you have done, He will forgive you and keep you after repentance. God loves you.

There is nothing good that will come out of trying to hide your sins. Proverb 128:13 says, *"He that covereth his sins shall not prosper: but whoso confesseth and forsaketh them shall have mercy."*

Chapter 16

Swear by Your Sin

One of the kings of Israel built images for the people. These images were given names, and the people accepted them as a part of their "religion." Whether they were coerced by the king to worship these images or whether they had become wicked on their own, they were yet still accountable for their actions. They had turned away from God.

Jeroboam, the king of Israel, built images of calves to be their god. These images were place strategically for the people to worship. Traditionally, the people would go to Jerusalem to the temple to worship three times a year. The images the king made were built and placed in the city of Dan. They were placed there so the people (rich or poor) would not have to travel all the way to Jerusalem to worship where the temple was located. Dan was about half the distance to Jerusalem.

In Amos 8:14, Amos explains what the Israelites had done: *"They that swear by the sin of Samaria, and say, Thy god, O Dan, liveth; and, The manner of Beersheba liveth; even they shall fall, and never rise up again."* The swearing implies they stated very strongly or sincerely that they would adhere to the newly created "gods" that were placed in the city. They used that location and the devices (images) they had created as their gods to worship in place of the true God.

Gill's Exposition of the Entire Bible explains how the Israelites swore by their sin:

> They that swear by the sin of Samaria ... The calf at Bethel, which was near Samaria, and which the Samaritans worshipped; and was set up by their kings, and the worship of it encouraged by their example, and which is called the calf of Samaria, Hosea 8:5; the making of it was the effect of sin, and the occasion of leading into it, and ought to have been had in detestation and abhorrence, as sin should; and yet by this the Israelites swore, as they had used to do by the living God; so setting up this idol on an equality with him: and say, thy God, O Dan, liveth; the other calf, which was set up in Dan; and to this they gave the epithet of the bring God, which only belonged to the God of Israel.

They swore or took an oath to worship the images the king had created. This was an action of sin: disobeying God and putting other "gods" before Him.

For man's disobedience, the Lord has made mercy available. God has mercy for man, but many times man seeks deliverance from self-invented forms which cannot benefit him in his spiritual life, as in this case of the Israelites. God gave man the ability and skill to make and create things, but He did not grant man permission to worship them or use their creations as a substitute for Him.

The Word of God tells us there should be no other gods before Him. Exodus 20:3 states, *"Thou shalt have no other gods before me."* Exodus 23:13, *"And in all things that I have said unto you be circumspect: and make no mention of the name of other gods, neither let it be heard out of thy mouth."* Deuteronomy 5:7 says, *"Thou shalt have none other gods before me."*

However, this act of the Israelites worshiping these images was futile. It was to no avail because there is one and only one God; that is the Lord God. There cannot be any god before Him or after him. He is the Alpha and the Omega, the beginning and the end.

Swearing on the sin you commit is rebellion against God and ignores what He has provided for us to live a righteous life. Hebrews 12:1-4 explain what all should do if they strays away from God. Jesus brought the solution.

> *Wherefore seeing we also are compassed about with so great a cloud of witnesses, let us lay aside every weight, and the sin which doth so easily beset us, and let us run with patience the race that is set before us, Looking unto Jesus the author and finisher of our faith; who for the joy that was set before him endured the cross, despising the shame, and is set down at the right hand of the throne of God. For consider him that endured such contradiction of sinners against himself, lest ye be wearied and faint in your minds. Ye have not yet resisted unto blood, striving against sin.*

Today, our Lord and Savior Jesus Christ is on the right hand of the throne of God and in our hearts. He is the Author and Finisher of our faith. Thus, we should live a committed life to Him because He died and rose and bore all sin. This, no other "god" has done; no object, no man, no pagan has done this. Therefore, the Lord God is the only living and true God.

The living God, our God does not ask much from us and no more than what He requires of us. If one dedicates or commits himself to serving other gods, he negates what is needed to render service to God. What is required of us in serving and worshiping God is explained in Micah 6:8. "*He hath shewed thee, O man, what is good; and what doth the Lord require of thee, but to do justly, and to love mercy, and to walk humbly with thy God?*" This means one is to be just/righteous, have love and mercy, and walk with Him humbly in the spirit at all times.

No matter what object, person or thing man may swear to worship and praise, it will be to no avail. Because God is the only one from whom man can receive salvation, mercy, forgiveness and eternal life. Jesus Christ has made this so easy for us to obtain by simply asking. 1 John 1:9 states, *"If we confess our sins, he is faithful and just to forgive us our sins, and to cleanse us from all unrighteousness."*

Chapter 17

Sin of My Soul

In order to live a righteous life, it is important for you to know what God requires of you. Knowing what is required of you correlates to your life's purpose. Everything in existence has a purpose. Without knowing the purpose of a thing, it cannot be used to the fullest of its capacity.

Man was created by God. Thus, man has a purpose like everything else God created. Knowing one's purpose is advantageous for his being. Purpose will help man maintain a righteous life while he is on this earth. Life is short and is destined to end. Purpose helps man to seek out what is needed to fulfill his destiny.

Man has been supplied the greatest tool in his life to carry out his purpose – the Word of God through biblical scriptures. His word nourishes, provides, leads, encourages, comfort, inspires, shapes character, gives peace, and loves- just to name a few.

Although man has the tool to prevent himself from sinning, unfortunately, he does not use this tool to maximize his resistance from sin. Scripture says all have sinned and come short of the glory of God. But when one sins what does he do?

In the book of Micah, Micah, who was a contemporary of Isaiah and Hosea, prophesied concerning both Israel and Judah. He took the message to the people admonishing them about the coming judgment, the future kingdom and their turning back to serving the Lord thy God. They had their ears open but did not hear or adhere to the warning. One would think they would have learned from their past experiences, but none listened.

In Micah 6:3-4, God raised the question about what He had done to them and why they continued to sin against Him. He mentioned some of the most noted things He had done for them: *"O my people, what have I done unto thee? And wherein have I wearied thee? testify against me. For I brought thee up out of the land of Egypt, and redeemed thee out of the house of servants; and I sent before thee Moses, Aaron, and Miriam."*

Micah, as well as Isaiah, prophesied the judgment that would be brought on by God. God knew their guilt, and the people themselves knew what they had done. Thus, the people wanted to clean themselves from all of their sin. Consequently, because of their ignorance, they wanted to pay for their guilt of sin with part of the wealth they had accumulated. Sin can easily bring on ignorance of the Word of God and how to properly deal with deliverance from sinful living. They had developed no appreciation for God or what He had done or what He required of them.

However, they did raise the question about what they should give for the sins of their soul. This was pointed out in Micah 6:7: *"Will the Lord be pleased with thousands of rams, or with ten thousands of rivers of oil? Shall I give my firstborn for my transgression, the fruit of my body for the sin of my soul?"* They had been turned away from God for so long until they had no inclination about what to do or how to rid the "sin of their soul." They knew not their purpose or what was required of them.

The Israelites suggested they give a thousand rams or ten thousands rivers of oil or even their firstborn for the sins they had committed. However, sin cannot be paid for by things. Sin can only be forgiven and then repented for. God wants you to give, but not in the way they proposed to please Him.

God, the judge, does not want sacrifices; He wants obedience. Scripture says obedience is better the sacrifice. The people had been offering burnt offerings for centuries, but God wanted more than that from them. He expressed His dissatisfaction with the offering they were making in Isaiah 1:11: *"To what purpose is the multitude of your sacrifices unto me? saith the* LORD: *I am full of the burnt offerings of rams, and the fat of fed beasts; and I delight not in the blood of bullocks, or of lambs, or of he goats."* Offering part of their wealth would not make up for the sins of their souls. Sin is to be forgiven by God, not paid for by man's possessions. Jesus Christ paid the price for our sins through atonement with His life. Jesus is the answer on how to deal with sin.

God wants you to give more than just material sacrifices. However, that is what some believers do sometimes; they make the necessary contribution to the ministry to help sustain it. Although financially this is needed, you cannot overlook the spiritual aspect of giving because it can have a profound effect on overcoming sin. God loves the "lip sacrifices," as Hebrew 13:15 states. *"Believers by him therefore let us offer the sacrifice of praise to God continually, that is, the fruit of our lips giving thanks to his name."*

Today, believers are required to live at a certain standard to meet what is required of them by God. Believers today also are under grace and led by the Holy Spirit via Christ Jesus. Quest Study Bible explains so clearly what is required:

> God want his people to live life that measure up to his moral and ethical standards. Through faith in Christ's death, not good works, God graciously saves us from the penalty of sin and makes peace with us. But that's not the end of the story. He saved us so that we might do good

deeds that exhibit God's character (Eph. 2:8-10). He wants us to treat others fairly and compassionately; he wants us to live humble, obedient lives.

Many of God's people failed to live up to God's high standards in Micah's time. God had delivered the Israelites from Egypt and established them as a nation. He called them to be a model society that would attract other nations to him (Deut.3:5-6). Instead they exploited the poor, selfishly pursuing their own interests. They rebelled against God's authority and rejected his prophets.

Despite their crimes, many Israelites actually thought their sacrifices made them pleasing to God. Micah attacked their faulty thinking. Empty ritual (vv.6-7) means nothing to God, Micah said. God wants lives of genuine ethical and moral integrity (Zondervan, 2003, p.1336).

Their way of thinking had been manifested because of prolonged sinful ways and not recognizing what God required of them. Micah 6 verse 8 explains what is needed: *"He hath shewed thee, O man, what is good; and what doth the Lord require of thee, but to do justly, and to love mercy, and to walk humbly with thy God?"* This is just part of what believers are to do.

The Israelites thought they could pay God off. God wanted them to seek forgiveness and walk in obedience. He also told them how to walk in obedience, which applies to all of today's believers. Once an earnest heart seeks the Lord, He will issue deliverance. Micah 7:8-9 declare how God will deliver you and shine the light on the path for all to walk by. *"Rejoice not against me, O mine enemy: when I fall, I shall arise; when I sit in darkness, the Lord shall be a light unto me. I will bear the indignation of the Lord, because I have sinned against him, until he plead my cause, and execute judgment for me: he will bring me forth to the light, and I shall behold his righteousness."*

One of the main characteristics of a believer is that he should always walk in the spirit, so his soul will not become infected with sin; one, then, can say that there is no sin of my soul. Scripture tells us in Galatians 5:25: *"If we live in the Spirit, let us also walk in the Spirit."* This Spirit is the Holy Spirit that dwells inside of you. Galatians 5:16 explains to us: *"This I say then, Walk in the Spirit, and ye shall not fulfill the lust of the flesh."* It is awesome to know that walking in the spirit can prevent you from sinning. Roman 8:21 tell us, *"There is therefore now no condemnation to them which are in Christ Jesus, who walk not after the flesh, but after the Spirit."* Thus, keep your soul clean by walking in the spirit and let Jesus lead you all the way to heaven.

Your sin cannot be bought, revised, edited, polished, waivered, or replaced by an object. It can only be forgiven. The Israelites were guilty, and they needed to confess their guilt (sin). Micah made it clear to his people during that time they needed to go to God and live the life He has prescribed in His word; that is to *"to act justly and to love mercy and to walk humbly with God"* (Quest Study Bible, Micah 6:8). These words are just as alive today as they were in Micah's time.

To live as God has prescribed, you must first be saved. When you are saved, you must obey God's Word. However, you are saved by grace through faith and not through obeying the law. On the other hand, you cannot obey the law unless you are saved. Your religious words and deeds (Micah 6:8) mean nothing to God if you lack character wrought by the Holy Spirit as you yield to Him.

Chapter 18

Fountain for Sin

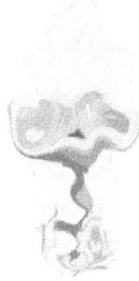

In the Old Testament, water was symbolic of cleansing away one's sin. This was an act of purification after defilement. When a person became unclean, he had to go through the ritual of cleansing himself in order for him to make sacrifices and worship God during that period. The unclean person would wash himself with purified water, and thus, he became clean again. This process was described in Numbers 19:9-22. The ritual they performed was purification from sin.

The elements involved in this purification were a heifer, ashes and water. Of the three elements, water was the substance that was doing the cleansing, and the other ones acted as catalysts.

This process used for purification of sin was a ritual but relevant to the teaching they received from their leaders at that time. These ceremonies were performed in accordance with the instruction of Moses; God spoke to him and gave him instruction for the people (Israelites) on what to do if they sinned or became unclean. God is a god of purity, cleanliness and holiness; He, therefore, expects His children to be the same.

Water is still used today in a ritualistic manner. It does not wash away sin as the Old Testament ritual reference. It, instead, symbolically represents the death, burial and resurrection of Jesus Christ. The process is called baptism. Water is used to baptize believers. It identifies a new life relationship with the Lord Jesus Christ where the death, burial and resurrection of Jesus are symbolized to draw one close to Him and fortify His belief.

There was another substance used in the Old Testament that was symbolic for cleansing one from sin: This was hyssop. Hyssop is a plant that will bare flowers twice a year. It became part of the Israelites' spiritual cleaning elements. It was used by dipping it in sacrificed blood (a lamb or heifer) and then sprinkled on the person being cleaned. David requested hyssop to be used to clean himself of his sins. Psalm 51:7 says, *"Purge me with hyssop and I shall be clean: wash me, and I shall be whiter than snow."* This was a symbolic cleansing of sin noted in Exodus 22 and Leviticus 14. The substances were merely a ritual that had been established but were used to reestablish a stronger relationship with God by admitting their guilt. However, only priests were allowed to perform these acts.

Then, there was the fountain that symbolizes spiritual cleansing from sin. A fountain is a structure that allows water to flow through it continuously. Running water is considered to be clean water because all impurities are washed downstream.

Zechariah prophesied the use of a fountain that our Lord and Savior Jesus Christ would set in place for dealing with sin. As stated in Zechariah 13:1: *"In that day there shall be a fountain opened to the house of David and to the inhabitants of Jerusalem for sin and for unclean-ness."*

The fountain's opening is a reference to the coming of the Messiah who would bring salvation and pave the way for a new life with the Holy Spirit to all believers. All of this had to come about with the shedding of Jesus Christ's blood on the cross. The shedding of His blood is the fountain of living water.

Zechariah pointed out specifically the sins of the people and how God would deal with the sin they had committed. Zechariah

13:2 says: *"And it shall come to pass in that day, saith the* LORD *of hosts, that I will cut off the names of the idols out of the land, and they shall no more be remembered: and also I will cause the prophets and the unclean spirit to pass out of the land."* These were sins the people of Israel were involved in, such as false prophets, idolatry, lying, lust and many more. However, these sins are prevalent today and need to be dealt with.

The fountain Zechariah prophesied to open is the fountain of living water. Jeremiah 2:13 references the fountain of living water and the Lord. *"For my people have committed two evils; they have forsaken me the fountain of living waters, and hewed them out cisterns, broken cisterns, that can hold no water."* The people had sinned and forsaken God. But only God himself can clean them of the evil sins they had committed against Him. The fountain of living water, which is our Savior, is available to all today. One only needs to receive Him and drink the "Living Water" He gives; one will not thirst any more.

Also in Jeremiah 17:13, God referred to himself as the fountain of living water when His people forsook Him. *"O* LORD, *the hope of Israel, all that forsake thee shall be ashamed, and they that depart from me shall be written in the earth, because they have forsaken the* LORD, *the fountain of living waters."*

The fountain is no longer seen in the sense that was used in the Old Testament. The fountain is seen as a fountain of living water characterized by Jesus Christ Himself. Jesus Christ is the source of this living water. It all came about through the sacrifice of Jesus on the cross. Jesus was sent and came to this world to save it from sin because sin is the work of the enemy (Satan), and Satan is out to destroy any good thing of God. This living water (the blood of Jesus) can wash away your sin.

Mathew Henry's Concise Commentary explains the relationship of the fountain of living water and Jesus Christ in Zechariah Chapter 13:

In the time mentioned at the close of the foregoing chapter, a fountain would be opened to the rulers and people of the Jews, in which to wash away their sins. Even the atoning blood of Christ, united with his sanctifying grace. It has hitherto been closed to the unbelieving nation of Israel; but when the Spirit of grace shall humble and soften their hearts, he will open it to them also. This fountain opened is the pierced side of Christ. We are all as an unclean thing. Behold a fountain opened for us to wash in, and streams flowing to us from that fountain. The blood of Christ, and God's pardoning mercy in that blood, made known in the new covenant, are a fountain always flowing, that never can be emptied. It is opened for all believers, who as the spiritual seed of Christ, are of the house of David, and, as living members of the church, are inhabitants of Jerusalem. Christ, by the power of his grace, takes away the dominion of sin, even of beloved sins. Those who are washed in the fountain opened, as they are justified, so they are sanctified. Souls are brought off from the world and the flesh, those two great idols that they may cleave to God only. The thorough reformation which will take place on the conversion of Israel to Christ is here foretold. False prophets shall be convinced of their sin and folly, and return to their proper employments. When convinced that we are gone out of the way of duty, we must show the truth of our repentance by returning to it again. It is well to acknowledge those to be friends, who by severe discipline are instrumental in bringing us to a sight of error; for faithful are the wounds of a friend, Proverbs 27:6. And it is always well for us to recollect the wounds of our Savior. Often has he been wounded by professed friends, nay, even by his real disciples, when they act contrary to His Word?

Therefore, instead of going through mere ceremonial cleansing, every believer should take part in the washing away of his/her sin via the blood of Christ. Peter explains this process. 1 Peter 1:2 says, *"According to the foreknowledge of God the Father, through sanctification of the Spirit, unto obedience and sprinkling of the blood of Jesus Christ: Grace unto you, and peace, be multiplied."*

The apostle John in the book of 1 John explains as believers walk in the light and the spirit and with one another, they are justified and cleansed by the blood of Jesus. 1 John 1:7 says, *"But if we walk in the light, as he is in the light, we have fellowship one with another, and the blood of Jesus Christ his Son cleanseth us from all sin."*

Jesus is Good All the Time

Jesus is good all the time.
He's always on my mind.
Jesus came and went away.
But yet and still, He is here to stay.
Jesus is good all the time.
When I am in trouble,
He will lead me through by showing me a sign.
He shines the light in my pathway.
He puts the right words in my mouth to say.
Jesus is good all the time.
I do what He says I should do, so I will not be left behind.
The Word says we are a chosen nation.
Jesus is the one who brought our salvation.
Jesus is good all the time.
He left His spirit for us to be filled.
He comforts us in times of sorrow and tears.
He makes us whole by washing our sins away.
We promise to Him no more will we sin.
Jesus is good all the time.
If you want to be saved and set free,
Open up your heart and let Him see.

Chapter 19

Declare Sin

As a prophet, Micah carried out the Lord's will openly and earnestly. He did not hesitate to make known the judgment against Israel. His prophecy or warning to the people took place sometime during the reigns of kings Johan, Ahaz, and Hezekiah.

All of his warnings were against the transgressions (sins) of the people of Israel (the northern kingdom) and Judah (the southern kingdom). In these nations, the people had become disobedient to the Word of God even though they had been taught right from wrong and what the Word of God commands for the way of life they should live.

The warning for judgment against Israel's leaders and the people were for their sin, and Micah explicitly describes in detail what they were doing. These sins were plotting evil, fraud, coveting, violence, stealing, dishonesty, evicting women from their homes, hating good, loving evil, despising justice, distorting what is right, murder, taking bribes, etc. All of the acts of sin can be found in Micah Chapters 2 and 3. These sins were declared by

Micah as stated in Micah 3: 8 *"But truly I am full of power by the spirit of the LORD, and of judgment, and of might, to declare unto Jacob his transgression, and to Israel his sin."*

These sins were declared, which means they were strongly stated by Micah as the sins of the people. When you declare something, you are basically confessing to a certain degree; you are expounding your belief and dedication about something you believe and support. In Micah 3, the transgressions and sins were declared. In other words, you are not trying to hide your sin or sweep them under the rug.

A declaration can be made upon anything. It does not have to be a sin or a transgression. You can declare righteousness, a declaration, or even a law. The essence of declaring is what you are serious about.

Psalm 38:13 makes a declaration; it says, *"For I will declare mine iniquity; I will be sorry for my sin."* This is David speaking declaring his sin. He humbly confesses his sins.

You must make a declaration to live a righteous life and seek the blood of Jesus for the atonement He made for you. Declare no more sin in your life. But declare a righteous life according to the Word of God.

Job says in 22:28, *"Thou shalt also decree a thing, and it shall be established unto thee: and the light shall shine upon thy ways."*

Chapter 20

Seven Deadly Sins

Sin is the most destructive device to mankind. It is the tool Satan uses to try to kill and destroy the very essence of man's existence. It, if allowed, will choke the life out of man, and it is used to coerce and recruit man to a life of disobedience to the Word of God.

However, it is important for one to know what sin is and how it operates in its attempt to destroy the righteousness of man. Righteousness is walking in the spirit and living according to the guidelines of God's Word.

There are literally hundreds of known sins that are open for man to fall into. There are seven sins listed in the Bible as seven sins that God really hates. God hates all sins, but these seven are noted because of their intensity. Perhaps even more so, it is because these seven sins engender other sins. What this means is other sins stem from these seven sins.

These seven sins that God hates are called the "seven deadly sins." They are called 'deadly' not because they would necessarily kill a person physically but can cause an eternal spiritual death.

These seven sins are explained in Proverb 6:16-19. These seven, which God hates, are an abomination to Him. Proverb 6:16-19 states, *"These six things doth the L*ORD *hate: yea, seven are an abomination unto him: A proud look, a lying tongue, and hands that shed innocent blood, An heart that deviseth wicked imaginations, feet that be swift in running to mischief, A false witness that speaketh lies, and he that soweth discord among brethren."*

In the Living Bible, Proverbs 6:16-19 states, *" For there are six things the Lord hates—no, seven: haughtiness, lying, murdering, plotting evil, eagerness to do wrong, a false witness, sowing discord among brothers."* Though the words are not as wordy as the King James Version, they express the same meaning.

For centuries, priests, preachers, teachers, scholars, and theologians have been pondering the meaning of these seven sins. The meaning is not difficult to understand, but their meaning has been extrapolated via several historic languages, which causes the name of a couple of the sins to vary in their description but not meaning. But, they all come today as seven simple meaning as explained as follows:

The first of the "deadly sins" is *"a proud look or haughtiness."* This is putting down others and elevating self above all. This sin makes one assume he/she has power when he/she does not. It is considering oneself more important than others. This sin stems from a lustful desire. Lust is an excessive desire that is usually associated with sex, but it can be an excessive desire involving money, power, fame or even food. God hates this.

The second "deadly sin" is *"a lying tongue."* Lying is distorting the truth. Without the truth, one cannot be free. A lying tongue is derived in a person for many reasons to falsely justify something or to try to make one free of guilt. However, the overall existence of a lying tongue is because the sinful nature of the person has overcome him or controls his inner being. There are severe consequences for a lying tongue. No treasures await one who lies. Proverb 21:6 points out the benefits of a person's lying tongue: *"The getting of treasures by a lying tongue is a vanity tossed to and fro of them that seek death."* A lying tongue distorts the Word of God. Psalm 109:2 says: *"For the mouth of the wicked and the mouth of the deceitful are opened against me: they have spoken against me with a lying tongue."* God hates a lying tongue.

The third "deadly sin" is *"hands that shed innocent blood."* This is simply the premeditated taking of a life. Of course, scripture tells us *"Thou shalt not kill"* in Exodus 20:13, which is part of the Ten Commandments delivered to the people of God by Moses. Not to kill another man is mentioned several times throughout the scriptures. Jesus expounded on 'not to kill' via the New Testament. Matthew 5:21 states: *"Ye have heard that it was said by them of old time, Thou shalt not kill; and whosoever shall kill shall be in danger of the judgment."*

Not to kill is referencing 'man' not animals or any other creature on earth. God created man and has put him head over all creatures. Therefore, man is of the utmost importance to Him, and He values the life of man. Thus, for a man to defy God's law, he is committing a sin. This is another sin that God hates.

The forth "deadly sin" is *"An heart that deviseth wicked imaginations."* Deviseth means to plan to obtain or bring about something – in this case 'to do evil.' This means a person has planned ahead to commit evil. Though the act of the sin is not committed yet, it is manifested as iniquity. The example of premeditated murder engenders this sin when a person plans to kill another. For example, David's sin of sending Uriah (Bashebia's husband) to the front line of battle, so he could be killed qualifies as this type of sin. David did this so he could take possession of

Uriah's wife. This was a sin devised to do evil. Though David did not actually kill him, he was responsible for his death via his wicked imagination and lust. He laid the foundation and structure for this sin to materialize.

The fifth "deadly sin" is *"feet that be swift in running to mischief."* This sin is when a person who indulges in sin is eager to commit it. He takes so much pleasure that he finds it hard to wait to do the respective sin. This person has no concern for righteousness and the consequences of sin even though he knows it is wrong. This person works iniquity with greediness.

The sixth "deadly sin" is *"A false witness that speaketh lies."* This sin comes down to a person who is a perpetual liar. He tells everything else but the truth. Obviously, a false witness has an ulterior motive behind his action. Usually, it is perpetrated for self-gain or pride; Proverbs explain how God feels about this type of action. Proverb 8:13 states, *"The fear of the LORD is to hate evil: pride, and arrogance, and the evil way, and the fraudulent mouth, do I hate."*

The seventh "deadly sin" is *"he that soweth discord among brethren."* This sin is an abomination to God. It attacks the essence of God, which is love. God is love, and He wants everyone to display and live a life of love; loving one another as brothers should. However, if one sows discord among his brothers, he is showing his lack of love and disdain to what the Word of God teaches us on how we should live. When there is discord among brothers, the Word of God is squeezed out and is separated from their lives. This discord causes division, and the focal point is placed on them instead of what God is teaching.

There should be no division among brothers. However, it is hard to find places where there is no division among brothers today. The Bible teaches unity. 1 Corinthians 1:10 teaches how men should live together as brothers. It states, *"Now I beseech you, brethren, by the name of our Lord Jesus Christ, that ye all speak the same thing, and that there be no divisions among you; but that ye be perfectly joined together in the same mind and in the same judgment."*

These "seven deadly sins" are sins that God hates, but it is important to know how they are manifested or moreover, their off-spring. Also, you should know the consequences for committing such acts. Galatians 5:19-21 explains what they are: *"Now the works of the flesh are manifest, which are these; adultery, fornication, uncleanness, lasciviousness, idolatry, witchcraft, hatred, variance, emulations, wrath, strife, seditions, heresies, envyings, murders, drunkenness, revellings, and such like: of the which I tell you before, as I have also told you in time past, that they which do such things shall not inherit the kingdom of God."*

The sins that are mentioned in these passages are all against the Word of God. The first six say that God hates them and the last one, which is, *"A false witness that speaketh lies, and he that soweth discord among brethren"* is an abomination to God. God hates all sins, whether considered to be big or small by man or premeditated or considered "innocent." God hates sin. All sin is an abomination to Him; abomination is expressing extreme disgust and hatred. Sin is hated by God.

As brothers and sisters and believers in the true God of our life, we all know that to sin is to oppose God in what He wants man to do while we live as visitors in this world. God has set the guidelines through His word of how man should live and conduct his life. To not do what He has prescribed in the way man should live creates a disconnection in man's relationship with Him. A healthy relationship with Him is free from perpetuating hatred or causing the wrath of God to come upon you. Man should become a "new creature" through the Word of God. The love of God's Word and the obedience to His word will prevent one from becoming an abomination to Him.

Let us all shun such practices as the "seven deadly sins" and watch and pray against them, avoiding them whenever possible.

We must use the Spirit in us to direct us away from the one who causes sin (Satan) against the Word of God.

Theme Verses for Each Chapter

Chapter 1
Isaiah 6:7 *"And he laid it upon my mouth, and said, Lo, this hath touched thy lips; and thine iniquity is taken away, and thy sin purged."*

Chapter 2
Isaiah 30:1 *"Woe to the rebellious children, saith the Lord, that take counsel, but not of me; and that cover with a covering, but not of my spirit, that they may add sin to sin:"*

Chapter 3
Isaiah 53:10 *"Yet it pleased the LORD to bruise him; he hath put him to grief: when thou shalt make his soul an offering for sin, he shall see his seed, he shall prolong his days, and the pleasure of the LORD shall prosper in his hand."*

Chapter 4
Jeremiah 16:1 *"And it shall come to pass, when thou shalt shew this people all these words, and they shall say unto thee, Wherefore hath the Lord pronounced all this great evil against us? or what is our iniquity? or what is our sin that we have committed against the Lord our God?"*

Chapter 5
Jeremiah 17:1 *"The sin of Judah is written with a pen of iron, and with the point of a diamond: it is graven upon the table of their heart, and upon the horns of your altars."*

Chapter 6
Jeremiah 31:34 *"And they shall teach no more every man his neighbour, and every man his brother, saying, Know the Lord: for they shall all know me, from the least of them unto the greatest of them, saith the Lord: for I will forgive their iniquity, and I will remember their sin no more."*

Chapter 7
Ezekiel 3:20 *"Again, When a righteous man doth turn from his righteousness, and commit iniquity, and I lay a stumbling block before him, he shall die: because thou hast not given him warning, he shall die in his sin, and his righteousness which he hath done shall not be remembered; but his blood will I require at thine hand."*

Chapter 8
Daniel 9:20 *"And whiles I was speaking, and praying, and confessing my sin and the sin of my people Israel, and presenting my supplication before the Lord my God for the holy mountain of my God."*

Chapter 9
Hosea 4:8 *"They eat up the sin of my people, and they set their heart on their iniquity."*

Chapter 10
Ezekiel 18:24 *"But when the righteous turneth away from his righteousness, and committeth iniquity, and doeth according to all the abominations that the wicked man doeth, shall he live? All his righteousness that he hath done shall not be mentioned: in his trespass that he hath trespassed, and in his sin that he hath sinned, in them shall he die."*

Chapter 11
Hosea 12:8 *"And Ephraim said, yet I am become rich, I have found me out substance: in all my labours they shall find none iniquity in me that were sin."*

Chapter 12
Hosea 13:2 *"And now they sin more and more, and have made them molten images of their silver, and idols according to their own understanding, all of it the work of the craftsmen: they say of them, Let the men that sacrifice kiss the calves."*

Chapter 13
Hosea 8:11 *"Because Ephraim hath made many altars to sin, altars shall be unto him to sin."*

Chapter 14
Nehemiah 1:6 *"Let thine ear now be attentive, and thine eyes open, that thou mayest hear the prayer of thy servant, which I pray before thee now, day and night, for the children of Israel thy servants, and confess the sins of the children of Israel, which we have sinned against thee: both I and my father's house have sinned."*

Chapter 15
Hosea 13:12 *"The iniquity of Ephraim is bound up; his sin is hid."*

Chapter 16
Amos 8:14 *"They that swear by the sin of Samaria, and say, Thy god, O Dan, liveth; and, The manner of Beersheba liveth; even they shall fall, and never rise."*

Chapter 17
Micah 6:7 *"Will the Lord be pleased with thousands of rams, or with ten thousands of rivers of oil? shall I give my firstborn for my transgression, the fruit of my body for the sin of my soul?"*

Chapter 18
Zechariah 13:1 *"In that day there shall be a fountain opened to the house of David and to the inhabitants of Jerusalem for sin and for uncleanness."*

Chapter 19
Micah 6:7 *"Will the Lord be pleased with thousands of rams, or with ten thousands of rivers of oil? shall I give my firstborn for my transgression, the fruit of my body for the sin of my soul?"*

Chapter 20
Proverb 6:16-19 *"These six things doth the LORD hate: yea, seven are an abomination unto him: A proud look, a lying tongue, and*

hands that shed innocent blood, An heart that deviseth wicked imaginations, feet that be swift in running to mischief, A false witness that speaketh lies, and he that soweth discord among brethren."

List of Commonly Committed Sins
and their Causes

*Bible verses used from ESV, NIV, KJV, and Topical Bible.

abandonment	Psalm 34:18; Psalm 27:10
abduction	Deuteronomy 24:7
abhorring judgment	Leviticus 26:43-44; Romans 2:1
	Psalm 26:5
abomination	Leviticus 20:13
abortion	Exodus 20:21-25
abusiveness	2 Peter 1:4
abhorrence of holy things	Act 2:33
accusation	Jude 1:9
adulterous lust	Matthew 5:27-28
adultery	Proverb 6:24-29; Proverb 6:32
afflicting others	Isaiah 58:1-14
aggravation	Genesis 2:24
agitation	Proverb 12:25
aiding and abetting sin	Colossians 3:12-17; 2 John 1:10
alcoholism	Galatians 5:21
all unrighteousness	1 John 1:9
anger	James 1:20
animosity	Ephesians 4:32
anxiety	Peter 5:6-7
apprehension	2 Thessalonians 1:1-12
argumentativeness	2 Timothy 2:15
arrogance	1Samuel 2:3
assaults	2 Samuel 13:1-39
astrology	Deuteronomy 28:9-12
atheism	Psalm 14:1
avariciousness	1 Timothy 6:9
Baal worship	2 Kings 17:16
backbiting	Proverbs 16:28; Romans 16:17:18

backsliding	2 Corinthians 13:5; Proverbs 14:14
bad attitude	Psalm 104:19
bad language	Ephesians 4:29
bearing false witness	Proverbs 19:5
big talk	Hebrews 10:25; Proverbs 10:19
being a workaholic	Proverbs 23:4; Proverbs 13:11
	Ecclesiastes 3:1-22
being too quick to speak	Proverbs 17:28
believing lies of the enemy	1 John 4:1; 2 Corinthians 11:13-15
belittling	Isaiah 55:8-9; Romans 15:1-33
bereavement	1 Thessalonians 4:13; John 5:28
betraying Jesus	Matthew 27:3; John 13:21
bickering	Philippians 2:14; Psalm 37:1-40
bigotry	Galatians 3:28; 1 Peter 2:1-25
bitterness	Ephesians 4:31-32; Proverbs 15:1
black magic	Deuteronomy 18:9-14
	Hebrews 13:8-9
blackmail	1 Corinthians 6:9-11
blaspheming the Holy Spirit	Matthew 12:31-32; Mark 3:29
boastfulness	Matthew 6:1-2; James 4:6
boisterousness	Exodus 23:1 1; Corinthians 6:9-10
bowing down to images	1 Timothy 2:5; Exodus 20:4-5
bragging	Matthew 6:1-34; Jude 1:16
	Jeremiah 9:23
brainwashing	Philippians 4:8; John 14:16
breaking God's commands	John 14:23-24; John 14:15
breaking God's covenants	Luke 22:30; 1 Corinthians 11:25
breaking covenants w/others	Hebrews 13:4; Genesis 2:14
bribery	Exodus 23:8; Proverb 15:27
	Proverb 17:23
brutality	Matthew 10:17-18; Revelation 20:4
burning incense to gods	Leviticus 10:1-2; Isaiah 1:13
calamity	Isaiah 45:7; Job 2:10
carelessness	2 Timothy 2:15; Joshua 1:8

cares & riches of this world	Matthew 6:24; 2 Corinthians 8:9
carnality	1 Corinthians 3:3; Romans 8:6
casting God away	1 John 4:1; 1 Chronicles 10:13-14
causing disagreements	Colossians 2:1-23
causing distress	2 Thessalonians 2:1-7
	Colossians 3:1-25
causing division	Romans 16:17-18; 2 Timothy 6:3-5
causing fear	John 14:27; 1 Peter 5:8
causing men to err	John 10:1-42; 1 Peter 1:22
causing offense	1 Corinthians 8:1-13
	2 Timothy 3:16
causing poor to fail	Luke 14:12-14; Luke 12:23
changing truth to lies	John 8:44; Ephesians 4:25
chanting of charms	Deuteronomy 18:9-12
	1 Corinthians 13:1-13
cheating	James 4:17; Hebrews 13:4
come against God's anointed	1 Samuel 24:6; 1 John 2:27
complaining	Philippians 2:14; Ephesians 4:29
complacency anti God's will	Proverb 1:23
	Hebrews 5:11-12
conceit	Romans 12:16; Jeremiah 9:23
	Proverb 26:12
concupiscence	Colossians 3:5; 1 Corinthians 13:8
condemnation	Roman 8:1; Romans 2:1-29
condemning the just	Ephesians 4:32; 1 Peter 3:8
causing conflict	Ephesians 4:32; 1 Peter 3:8
confrontation	Matthew 18:15:20; Galatians 6:1
confusion	2 Timothy 2:7; 1 Corinthians 14:33
conjuration	1 Timothy 4:1; 2 John 1:9-11
conspiring against God	Roman 13:1-14 Exodus 23:1
consulting wizards, psychics	Leviticus 19:31
	1 Chronicles 10:13-14
contempt	Romans 14:1-23
contention	Proverbs 3:30

controlling	2 Peter 1:5-8
conniving	Proverb 6:16-19; Exodus 20:16
compulsiveness	1 Corinthians 9:27
contentiousness	1 Corinthians 11:16
contesting and resisting God	1 Timothy 3:1-7; Roman 1:19
corruption	2 Peter 2:19; 1 Thessalonians 5:22
counterfeiting Christian work	2 Corinthians 11:13-15; John 8:44
covering sin	Roman 6:33; Proverbs 28:13
coveting	Exodus 20:17; Deuteronomy 5:22
covetousness	1 Timothy 6:6-11
cravenness	Proverbs 23:31
criticalness	Colossians 3:12-14
crookedness	Proverb 11:3; 2 Corinthians 4:4
cruelty	Proverb 12:10; Mark 9:43
using crystals	Acts 8:9-13
cursing God	Matthew 10:32-33
	Matthew 12:31:32
cursing	Ephesians 4:29; Ephesians 5:4
dealing treacherously	Romans 7:3; Hebrews 12:13
deceit	Proverbs 20:17; Psalm 101:17
deception	Galatians 6:7-8; Proverbs 10:9
defamation	Titus 3:1-2
defeatism	Ephesians 6:10-18
defiantness	Genesis 3:1-24
defiling	Leviticus 15:31; Numbers 6:9
degrading	Romans 1:24
dejection	Proverb 29:23
demon consciousness	Acts 16:16-18; Matthew 9:32-33
demon worship	Ephesians 6:10-13; Psalm 106:37
deny Jesus, His resurrection	Matthew 10:33
dependencies	1 Thessalonians 4:12; Leviticus 21:3
depravity	Romans 1:29; 2 Peter 2:19
desecration	Ezekiel 7:22; Deuteronomy 21:23
desires of this world	Colossians 3:5; Romans 12:2

despair	Isaiah 19:9; Isaiah 61:3
despising God	1 Samuel 2:30; 2 Samuel 12:9
despitefulness	Leviticus 20:13; Leviticus 18:22
despondency	Galatians 6:9; Revelation 21:4
deviousness	Proverb 2:16; Proverb 14:2
disagreements	Ephesians 4:31-5:2; Acts 15:36
disbelief	Mark 9:24; 2 Timothy 4:3-4
discord	Proverb 6:16-19; Esther 1:18
discrediting	2 Peter 1:21; 2 Timothy 3;16-17
discouragement	Exodus 6:9; Jeremiah 19:11
	Exodus 6:9
disdain	Proverb 23:22; Romans 13:1-7
disgust	Ezekiel 23:17; Ezekiel 23:18
dishonesty	Colossians 3:9-10; Proverb 20:17
	Exodus 20:16
disobedience	Deuteronomy 28:15; Hebrews 2:2
disorderly	2 Thessalonians 3:6; Romans 16:17
disputing	1 Timothy 2:8; Jude 1:9
disrespectfulness	1 Corinthians 15:33; Esther 1:18
disruptive	1 John 2:15; Ephesians 4:29
dissension	Proverb 6:14; Proverbs 15:18
	Romans 13:13
distantness	Deuteronomy 30:4; Matthews 25:41
distrust	2 Timothy 3:16; John 13:35
division	1 Corinthians 1:10-13; Luke 11:17
divorce	Deuteronomy 24:1;1 Corinthians7:15
domineering	Galatians 3:28; 1 Timothy 2:12
double-talking	1 Peter 5:8; 2 Corinthians 10:5
	Proverbs 6:12-16
double mindedness	James 1:6-8; James 4:8
doubt	Proverbs 3:5-8; James 1:6
dread	Deuteronomy 7:21; John 14:1
drug abuse	1 Corinthians 6:19-201
	Corinthians 3:17

drunkenness	Proverbs 20:1; Ephesians 5:18
duplicity	Proverbs 6:16-19; Romans 12:17-21
	Exodus 20:16
drinking blood	Genesis 9:304; Acts 15:20
eating blood	Deuteronomy 12:33
eating unclean food	Acts 10:14
effeminate behavior	Deuteronomy 6:9; Hebrews 13:4
egotism	Philippians 2:1-10; John 5:31
enchantment	Numbers 23:23; Leviticus 19:23
enlarged imaginations	2 Corinthians 10:5
	Revelation 22:1-21
enter unrighteous agreements	Hosea 10:4
envy (produced by lust)	Job 5:2; Proverbs 3:31; 23:17
escaping	1 Corinthians 10:13; Luke 21:36
	Acts 2:40
evil hearts & imaginations	2 Thessalonians 3:2; Romans 6:23
exasperation	Ephesians 4:1-3; Matthew 5:40
	Proverbs 12:156
extortion	Leviticus 6:4; Ecclesiastes 7:7
	Isaiah 33:15
failure in duty	Genesis 38:8; Acts 23:1 1
	Corinthians 7:3
failure to glorify God	Psalm 69:12, 86:12; Romans 15:9
falsehood	Job 21:34; Psalm 119:163
	1 John 4:6
fantasizing	James 1:14-15; 2 Timothy 2:22
fault finding	John 7:24; Matthew 7:1-5
fear	2 Timothy 1:7; 1 John 4:18
fear of disapproval	2 Kings 8:19; Nehemiah 6:16
	Proverbs 3:32
fear of man	Proverb 29:25
fetishes	Romans 7:8; James 1:14
	2 Peter 2:10
fighting	Proverb 28:25; Matthew 18:15

	Galatians 5:15
flattery	Proverbs 29:5; Job 32:21-22
foolishness	1 Corinthians 1:18, 1:23
folly	Job 42:8; Palm 69:5
forcefulness	Matthew 11:12; 2 Corinthians 10:10
fornication	1 Corinthians 7:2; 1 Corinthians 6:18
fortune telling	Leviticus 19:3
	1 Deuteronomy 18:10-12
fraud	Luke 16:10-13; Proverbs 20:17
	Jeremiah 10:14
fretting	1 Peter 5:5-7; 1 Peter 3:3-4
frustrations	2 Samuel 13:2; Nehemiah 4:15
fury	Job 40:11; Proverb 22:8
	Genesis 27:44
giving offense	Genesis 20:16
gloominess	Zephaniah 1:15; Daniel 12:1
gluttony	Proverbs 23:2; Philippians 3:19 1
	Corinthians 10:31
gossip	Proverbs 11:13, 20:19, 26:20
greed	Matthew 23:25; Luke 12:15
grieving	Nehemiah 8:10; 8:11
	Ephesians 4:30
grumbling	Exodus 16:7; Numbers 17:10
	John 6:43
guilt	Hosea 13:16; John 9:41; Hosea 5:15
harlotry	Nahum 3:4; Jeremiah 13:27;
	Hosea 5:4
harshness	Malachi 3:13; 2 Corinthians 13:10
hating God	Exodus 20:5
hating	Titus 3:3; Jude 1:23
haughtiness	Jeremiah 48:29
high-minded	1 Corinthians 1:19
homosexuality	1 Corinthians 6:9; Leviticus 18:22
hopeless	Isaiah 57:10

horoscopes	Leviticus 19:31; 1 John 4:1
human sacrifice	Deuteronomy 18:20
hypocrisy	Matthew 23:28; 1 Peter 2:1
idleness	2 Thessalonians 3:6; Proverbs 31:27
idle words, deeds, & actions	Matthew 12:36-37; Proverbs 18:8
idolatries	Jeremiah 14:14; 1 Corinthians 10:14
	Colossians 3:5
ignorance	Ephesian 4:18; 1 Timothy 1:13
ill will	Deuteronomy 15:9
inhumanity	1 John 3:15
imaginations	2 Corinthians 10:5
	Isaiah 65:2, 66:18
immorality	Jeremiah 3:9; Jude 1:4
impatience	James 5:7-8; Galatians 5:22
	Colossians 1:11
impetuousness	Habakkuk 1:6
imprudence	Proverbs 14:8, 14:15
impurity	Leviticus 15:19; Zechariah 13:1
inadequacy	2 Corinthians 12:9; Philippians 1:20
incest	Leviticus 18:6-18
	Deuteronomy 27:23
incitement	Proverbs 29:11
indifferences	Revelation 3:15-16
	Matthew 11:16-17
inflating	Matthew 7:1; John 11:26
inflexibility	Philippians 4:1-23
inhospitality	Ezekiel 16:49-50; Genesis 19:5
iniquity in your heart	Psalm 25:11; 51:9
injustice	Micah 6:8; Exodus 23:7
insolence	Titus 3:2; Proverbs 15:1
intemperance	Proverbs 23:29-35; 2 Timothy 1:7
intentional sins	Hebrews 10:26
intimidation	Nehemiah 6:13, 14, 19
intolerances	2 Samuel 12:7

intellectualism, sophisticated	1 Timothy 6:20; 1 Corinthians 1;27
inventing sin	James 1:4; Acts 2:28
inventing evil	Romans 1:24-32; Psalm 55:15
inward wickedness	Ephesians 6:12
irrationality	Roman 1:20; John 4:24
irreverence	Nehemiah 5:15; Jeremiah 44:10
jealousy	Exodus 34:14; Acts 7:9
being judgmental	Luke 6:37; John 12:48
justifying the wicked	Proverbs 11:1
kidnapping	Deuteronomy 24:7
killing	1 Samuel 19:5
lack of self-control	1 Corinthians 7:9
lawlessness	1 John 3:4; James 4:17
lasciviousness	Proverbs 2:16-18
laziness	Proverbs 12:24; Proverbs 19:16
lesbianism	Romans 1:27-27
levitation	Isaiah 60:1, 60:8
lewdness	Ephesians 5:5; 1 Corinthians 6:9-10
lying	Proverbs 12:22; 1 John 2:4
loathing	Psalm 119:158
longing for sin	1 Peter 2:1-25; 1 Timothy 2:1-15
loneliness	Psalm 25:16; Hebrews 13:5
loose morals	James 1:12; 2Timothy 2:15
looting	1 Samuel 23:1; Ephesians 4:28
loving evil	Psalm 52:3; Psalm 57:10
	Roman 12:9
loving money	Matthew 6:24; 1 Timothy 6:10
loving praise	Philippians 2:3-4
lust	Matthew 5:28; Galatians 5:16
lust of the eye	Matthew 5:28; 1 John 2:16
	Psalm 119:37
lust of the flesh	1 John 2:16
lust of the mind	Psalm 25:11; Psalm 38:18
lying to the Holy Spirit	Acts 5:1-5; Proverb 12:22

lying with pleasure & delight	Colossians 3:9-10; Proverbs 12:19
madness	John 10:20; Jeremiah 50:38
magic	Acts 8:9-13; Ezekiel 13:18
making war	Micah 3:5; Psalm 140:2; Job 38:23
maliciousness	Exodus 23:1; Proverbs 17:4
manipulation	Galatians 2:4; 2 Corinthians 11:20
manslaughter	Matthew 5:21; Exodus 23:7
marauding	Joshua 8:27; 1 Samuel 15:19
masturbation	James 1:14-15; 1 Corinthians 10:13
materialism	Luke 12:15; Matthew 6:19-21
mischief	Ephesians 4:1-3; Proverbs 12:16
misery	Exodus 3:7; Judges 10:16
misleading	Matthew 18:6-7; 2 Chronicles 32:15
mulishness	Leviticus 26:19; Psalm 81:12
mocking	Proverbs 17:5; 2 Peter 3:3-7
murder	Exodus 20:13; Numbers 35:12
murmuring	Philippians 2:14; James 5:8
muttering	Isaiah 8:19; Lamentations 3:62
necromancy	Leviticus 19:31; 1 John 4:1
negativism	Matthew 7:1-2; 2 Corinthians 10:5 Romans 15:5-6
nicotine addiction	1 Corinthians 6:19-20; 3:17
not being watchful	Matthew 24:24; John 4:48
occultism	Isaiah 8:18; 2 King 21:6
obsessing	2 Corinthians 10:4-5; Philippians 4:8
obstinacy	1 John 3:2; Hebrews 4:12
oppression	Deuteronomy 26:7; Job 35:9
overbearing	Titus 1:7
pedophilia	Leviticus 18:23, 20:12; Mark 9:42
persecuting believers	2 Timothy 3:12; John 15:18
persecuting, persecution	Acts 9:11; John 15:18; 1 Peter 3:14 Matthew 5:10
perversion	Leviticus 18:23; Romans 1:27
perverting the gospel	Acts 20:20; Galatians 1:7

petulance	Isaiah 40:32; Job 38:4
planning without God	Proverbs 16:9; Matthew 6:34
plotting	Ezekiel 11:2; Proverbs 16:30
plundering	Ezekiel 39:10
pompousness	1 Timothy 4:13; 1 John 4:6
pornography	Psalm 101:3; Proverbs 6:25-27
possessiveness	Mark 12:27; Malachi 3:17
	Ephesian 4:28
pouting	Proverbs 14:17, 15:18; James 1:19
prayerlessness	1 Thessalonians 5:17; John 15:7
	Philippians 4:6
prejudice	Galatians 3:28; Titus 1:12-13
	Ephesians 4:32
presumption	2 Peter 3:1-18; 1 Corinthians 2:14
pretending to be a prophet	2 Peter 2:1-22; 2 Timothy 3:16
pretension	2 Corinthians 10:5
pridefulness	Proverbs 11:2; Proverbs 29:23
pride of life	1 John 2:16; Proverbs 27:2
	Jeremiah 9:23
procrastination	1 Peter 5:7; Psalm 39:7
profane God, His holiness	Colossians 3:8; Ephesians 4:29
profanity unto God	1 Timothy 6:10; Psalm 34:13
professing to be wise	James 1:1-27
prophecy by Baal	Deuteronomy 18:15; Matthew 24:11
prophesying lies	1 John 4:1
propagating lies	Exodus 5:9; Proverbs 19:5
proudness	James 4:6; Proverbs 16:5
provoking God	Deuteronomy 4:25; 1 Kings 16:7
provoking	Galatians 5:26; Jeremiah 7:19
puffing up	1 Samuel 17:28; Galatians 5:26
	Colossian 2:18
quarreling	Genesis 13:8; 1 Corinthians 3
quenching the Holy Spirit	Solomon 8:7; Amos 5:6
questioning God's Word	Isaiah 55:8-9; 1 Corinthians 2:16

raiding	Proverbs 24:15
railing	Proverb 102.8
raging	Psalm 37:8; Romans 12:21
	Proverbs 15:1
raping	Deuteronomy 22:25-28; Psalm 82:3
rationalization	Luke 14:18-20; Genesis 3:13
ravaging	1 Chronicles 21:12; Acts 8:1-40
rebellion	Psalm 106.43; 1 Samuel 15:23
	Proverbs 17:11
rebuking	2 Timothy 3:16; Proverb 27:5
recklessness	Numbers 22:32; Judges 9:4
refusing to hear	Matthew 11:15; Exodus 19:9
refusing to repent	Jeremiah 15:19; 1 John 1:9
refusing to be humble	1 Chronicles 7:14; James 4:6
refusing to live in peace	Roman 5:1; Philippians 4:7
rejecting reproof, salvation	Proverbs 5:12, 6:23
rejecting God and His Word	Luke 9:23; Matthew 10:32
	Galatians 1:8-9
rejection	Romans 11:15; Hosea 4:6
	1 Peter 2:4
rejoicing in others' adversity	Colossians 2:18
rejoicing in idols	1 Corinthians 10:14
rejoicing in iniquity	John 14:1-31
repetitiveness	Hebrews 10:26
reproaching good men	Job 27:6; Proverbs 79:12
resentment	Judges 8:3; Job 5:2; Job 36:13
restlessness	Genesis 4:12; James 3:8
retaliation	Matthew 5:39; Matthew 6:15
reveling	1 Samuel 30:16; Isaiah 23:12
	2 Peter 2:13
reviling	Matthew 5:11, 15:4
revenge	Leviticus 19:18; Romans 12:19
rigidity	Mark 9:18; Matthew 11:28-39
robbing God	Malachi 3:8

robbery	Philippians 2:6; Isaiah 61:8
	Ezekiel 18:7
rudeness	Matthew 5:22; Proverbs 15:23
sadism	Nahum 3:19; Psalm 71:4
	Proverbs 11:17
scheming	Ester 9:25; Ezekiel 38:10
	Ecclesiastes 7:25, 27
scornfulness	1 Samuel 2:29; Psalm 64:8
	Galatians 4:14
seduction	Acts 18:13; Habakkuk 1:3
seeking self-gain	Matthew 6:33; Psalm 27:8
seek pleasures from world	Matthew 6:33; 1 Chronicles 22:19
self-accusations	1 Corinthians 3:16-17
self-admiration	1 Corinthians 3:16-17
self-centeredness	Matthew 16:24
self-condemnation	1 Peter 3:3-4; Matthew 16:24-25
	Roman 8:1-2
self-corruption	Luke 16:15; Roman 12:3
self-criticalness	Proverbs 12:18
self-deception	2 Peter 3:9; Acts 14:15
self-delusion	Titus 1:11-12; Romans 8:7-9
self-destruction	Matthew 7:13-14; Psalm 97:2-7
self-exultation	Isaiah 45:25; Isaiah 14:8
self-glorification	Psalm 34:3; Psalm 69:30
self-hatred	Ephesians 5:29; Proverbs 10:18
	Proverbs 10:12
self-importance	Galatians 2:6; Mark 12:29
self-rejection	Psalm 34:17-20; Romans 8:1, 12:10
selfishness	Philippians 2:4; Galatians 6:2
self-pity	1 Thessalonians 5:18; James 5:13
self-righteousness	Luke 18:9-14; Matthew 6:7
self-seeking	Romans 2:8; 1 Corinthians 13:4-5
serving other gods	Joshua 24:15
sewing discord	Proverbs 6:16-19; Exodus 20:16

sexual idolatry	Matthew 5:28 1 Thessalonians 4:2-8
sexual immorality	1 Thessalonians 4:2-8 1 Corinthians 6:18-20
sexual impurity	1 Thessalonians 4:3-5 Galatians 5:19-21
sexual perversion	Leviticus 18:23; 20:13; Jude 1:7
oral sex	1 Corinthians 7:3-4; Solomon 2:3
sodomy	Leviticus 20:13; Romans 1:26
shame	Isaiah 61:7; Psalm 34:4-5
silliness	Proverbs 8:5; Romans 16:24
sinful mirth	Job 20:5
skepticism	Matthew 21:21; James 1:6
slander	Leviticus 19:16; Psalm 54:5 Proverbs 10:18
slaying	Psalm 34:21; Genesis 37:26
slothfulness	Proverbs 6:6; 19:15; Colossians 3:17
snobbishness	Romans 12:16; Psalm 2:1-22
soothsaying	Leviticus 20:6 Acts 19:19
sorcery	Leviticus 19:31; 1 Chronicles 10:13
sowing seeds of hatred	James 4:11; Proverbs 6:14
speaking curses	Isaiah 8:10; Jeremiah 48:10
speaking incantations	Ezekiel 13:20; Revelation 21:8
speaking folly	Job 42:8; Psalm 38:5 Proverbs 12:23
speculation	Matthew 12:37; Proverbs 13:3
spell-casting	Matthew 10:28; 1 Corinthians 2:11
spiritual laziness	Proverbs 19:16; Proverbs 13:4
spitefulness	1 Peter 2:1-25; 1 Timothy 2:1-15
stealing	Ephesians 4:28; Proverbs 10:23
stiff-necked	Exodus 32:9; Deuteronomy 10:16
strife	Proverbs 20:3; Proverbs 17:1
striving over leadership	Colossians 3:23-24; Acts 20:28
struggling	1 Corinthians 10:13; Romans 8:18

stubbornness	Psalm 81:11-12; Romans 2:5
stupidity	Romans 1:22; Proverbs 12:1
	Proverbs 14:16-18
suicidal thoughts	James 4:7; 1 Corinthians 3:16-17
	Ecclesiastes 7:17
suspicion	Hebrews 11:6; Proverbs 3:5
swearing	James 5:12; Matthew 5:34-37
taking advantage of others	Luke 6:31; 1 Thessalonians 4:6
taking a bribe	Exodus 23:8; Deuteronomy 16:19
taking offense	1 Samuel 25:28; Job 10:14,13:23
taking God's Name in vain	Matthew 12:23
taking rights from poor	Ezekiel 18:16,18
teaching false doctrines	1 Timothy 1:3, 6:3
temper	1 Samuel 20:7; Proverbs 16:32
temptation	Matthew 6:13, 26:14
tempting God	James 1:13
theft	Matthew 15:19
timidity	2 Timothy 1:7
trickery, two-facedness	Genesis 3:1; Matthew 24:24
trustless	Numbers 20:12
trusting lies	Psalm 118:8; Galatians 6:3
trusting own righteousness	John 14:1; Jeremiah 48:7
trusting wickedness	John 12:36
tumults	Amos 2:2; Galatians 1:7, 5:10
turning your back on God	Matthew 10:33; Ephesians 6:11
unbelief	Mark 9:24; Romans 4:20
unbridled lust	1 Thessalonians 4:4
uncleanness	Matthew 12:43; Ezekiel 44:23
uncompromising	James 4:17; Galatians 5:16
undermining	Job 15:4
unequal yoked no-believers	2 Corinthians 6:14
unfairness	Matthew 20:13
unfaithfulness	Leviticus 6:2; Deuteronomy 32:20
unforgiveness	Mark 11:25

unfriendliness	Proverbs 18:1
ungratefulness	Luke 6:35; 2 Timothy 3:2
unholy alliances	1 Kings 3:1; Isaiah 30:1
unholy habits	1 Timothy 5:13; Hebrews 10:25
unmanly	Genesis 1:26
unmercifulness	Matthew 18:21; Jude 1:22
unrepentant	1 John 1:9; Revelation 2:5
unrighteousness	Jeremiah 22:13; Romans 3:5
	1 John 1:9
unruliness of tongues	Micah 6:13; Psalm 120:2
usury	Nehemiah 5:10; 5:7; Psalm 15:5
	Ezekiel 18:13
unthankful	Colossians 3:15, 4:2
untruthfulness	Proverbs 12:17, 14:5
Unworthiness	Luke 17:10; 1 Corinthians 11:27
using tarot cards	Leviticus 20:6; Mark 13:1-37
vain imaginations	Zachariah 10:2; Philippians 2:3
vanity	1 Samuel 16:7; Ecclesiastes 5:10
vengeance	Romans 12:19; Matthew 5:38-39
viciousness	Matthew 26:52-54; Psalm 11:5
violence	Job 16:17; Obadiah 1:10
vulgarity	Ephesians 4:29, 5:4
	1 Thessalonians 5:22
white magic	Leviticus 19:31; 1 John 4:1
wickedness	1 Timothy 5:8; Ezekiel 33:11
willful sin	Hebrews 10:26; 1 John 3:4
willful and/or intentional sin	Numbers 3:1-51; Hebrews 10:26
winking with evil intent	Job 15:12; Proverbs 3:29
witchcraft, withdrawal	Deuteronomy 18:9-12, 18:20
	Micah 5:12
withholding a pledge	Proverb 3:27, 23:13
without concern	1 Timothy 6:20; Acts 24:23
without natural affection	John 13:34-35; Ephesians 4:31-32
without mercy	Luke 6:36; Matthew 5:7

working for praise	Galatians 5:16-26; 1 John 2:16
	Galatians 6:7-9
worldliness	1 John 2:15-17; Romans 12:2
worrying	Matthew 6:25-34; 1 Peter 5:7
	Matthew 10:19
worshipping possessions	Revelation 9:20; 1 John 2:15-17
worshipping our works	Romans 1:25
worshipping the creation	Romans 1:25
worshipping of planets	John 4:23
wrathfulness	Psalm 37:8; Romans 12:19
wrong doing	Exodus 23:2; Isaiah 1:16
zealous to make others sinful	Romans 10:2
zealousness in outward show	Philippians 1:27

References

Bible Gateway. Biblegateway.com. July 2014.

Bible Hub. Biblehub.com. August 2014.

Biblestudytools.com. September 2014.

Children bible story book. Lavistachurchofchrist.com.

Christ Notes. Christnotes.org. December 2014.

"Confessing." Merriam-Webster Dictionary. http://www.merriam-webster.com. December 2014.

Gill. J. *Gill's Exposition of the Entire Bible.* www.ewordtoday.com/comments/gill. July 2014.

Good News Translation. biblegateway.org.

Henry, M. *Matthew Henry's Commentary* www.Christnotes.org.

High Calling Ministries. http://www.thehighcalling.org

Openbible.info

Tyndale. (2003). *Life Application Study Bible* (KJV).

"Wicked." Dictionary.com. January 2015.

Wiersbe, W. W. *Bible Commentary*. (1991).Thomas Nelson Publishers.

WorldNet (r) 1.7. http://dictionary.die.net/fear

Zondervan. (2003). *NIV Quest Study Bible, Revised*. Grand Rapids, Michigan 49530.

About the Author

Minister Rayford Jones Elliott is a minister of the gospel of Jesus Christ. He is a devout follower of Christ Jesus because he loves the Lord with his whole heart. As a minister, he teaches and preaches the Word with great fervency in an attempt to save the lost by bringing them into the knowledge of the truth. In his local church, where he has been a member for thirteen years, Minister Elliott serves as the president of the Men's Fellowship. He conducts weekly discussion groups thereby demonstrating his dedication to spiritual development of men. It is his desire to instill in them the same love and zeal for Christ Jesus that he possesses.

www.ingramcontent.com/pod-product-compliance
Lightning Source LLC
LaVergne TN
LVHW051136080426
835510LV00018B/2445